standing in death's shadow
MORE TRUE STORIES FROM A HOMICIDE DETECTIVE

KEN LANG

KEN LANG STUDIOS

Copyright 2011 Ken Lang

standing in death's shadow is a work of non-fiction . Names places, dialog, and identifying details have been changed.

Edited by: Brenda Coxe - bscoxe@comcast.net

ISBN-13: 978-1475291667
ISBN-10: 1475291663

KEN LANG STUDIOS
www.KenLangStudios.com

To the men and women who tirelessly seek justice
for those who are unable speak for themselves.

standing in death's shadow

MORE TRUE STORIES FROM A HOMICIDE DETECTIVE

CHAPTER ONE

After finally reaching her driveway, Edith pushed the gear selector into park and drew in a long deep breath. She had just endured a 12-hour shift she at the restaurant, it felt good to be off her feet. While Wednesdays were always busy, perhaps for the convenience of hustling families with midweek activities, Edith was thankful she would have a few hours to recline in front of her television before dragging her weary body off to bed.

Edith wormed her way from the driver's seat, throwing her weighted purse over her shoulder. She fumbled through her keys in the darkness of the late night as she meandered to the rear kitchen door and placed the key into the dead-bolt lock. Turning the key, she felt the empty slack in the deadbolt announcing that the door was already unsecured. *That's strange,* she thought as she gave the knob a twist and pushed on the door.

Edith swung open the door when her effort came to an abrupt halt, only gapping a few meager inches.

"What the hell?" Edith said aloud to herself. Leaning in with her shoulder, she pressed hard against the door, muscling it open just enough for her to squeeze through the narrow cavity.

Wiggling through the entryway, she could barely see the

looming object lying at her feet. She reached for the light switch, flipped it up, and illuminated the darkened room to see what was causing her weary muscles to ache even more.

"Oh, God! Oh, God!" she yelled, tripping over Darlene's lifeless body. Blood stretched across the scuffed linoleum floor pooling where it poured from the partially exposed wounds. No need to reach down and check Darlene's well-being; the empty stare confirmed her demise.

Stunned and dismayed, Edith stumbled in place, unsure what her next move should be. Surveying the scene in horror, her heart felt as if it had dropped right out of her chest. Her ears tuned into quieted movement lumbering towards her from the living room's darkened corridor.

"Harold?" she called out. The shadow now stood in the dining room, a butcher knife clenched in his lowered right hand.

"Yeah, Mom," the shadow answered.

"What the hell is going on?"

"I don't know, Mom... I don't know."

Harold turned and walked back through the living room, found his way through the front door, stopped in the front yard, and pulled out his cell phone. Even more confused than when she initially found Darlene's cadaver at her back door, Edith followed her son, taking careful measures not to step in the puddles of drying blood and track it onto her light gray carpet

Edith leaned out the front door and braced herself on the screen door's handle as she cried out to Harold.

"Harold! Who the hell are you talking to? What is going on?" she demanded.

Harold folded the cell phone, sliding it into his pocket before climbing into his little blue hatchback. Driving off into the night, he sensed deep within his spirit he would never see his mother again.

****

In only a matter of minutes Edith was able to collect her

wits and notify 911 of her horrific discovery. The patrol officers working the district immediately flooded the residence with their presence, their curiosity taking in the ghastly scene. Securing a perimeter around the two-story white bungalow converted into apartments, the officers tied the crime scene tape and stationed a sentry at the main entrance. Extracting his lookout book from his back left pocket, the officer initiated the official documentation for the investigation.

Receiving notification twenty minutes earlier, detectives descended upon the confined address, leaving behind any possibility of getting off on time from this evening shift stint.

"Yates, you're going to be lead on this one," the sergeant directed. "Lang and Gibson, you're his support. Anything he needs, be sure he gets it."

Yates extracted a reporter's style notebook from his jacket pocket and flipped open the front cover, exposing a pristine white page. He knew how important this investigation would be and noted relevant information he would need to draw on later to identify his suspect. After all, this was his first murder investigation as a lead detective since his assignment to the unit two months ago.

Filing in through the front door, Yates, Lang, and Gibson found themselves in a well-lit living room where Edith sat nervously shaking on the living room couch. As Yates walked towards Edith, his eyes focused on the bloodstains on the arm of the recliner situated close to the couch.

"Edith, I'm Detective Yates. Tell me, what happened tonight?"

Edith sat on the edge of the couch, her hands clenching a wad of tissues. "I'm not sure," she answered softly. "I came home from work and found Darlene lying dead inside my kitchen door. Then my son, Harold, came around the corner... he was holding a bloody butcher knife in his hand." As Edith's tears streamed down her cheek, she buried her face in a mass of Kleenex, concealing her shame.

Lang and Gibson wandered around the corner, in through the dining room, stopping at the entrance to the kitchen. *Might need some booties,* Lang thought, taking in the scene. Darlene was still lying face up, her blank stare focused on the ceiling above her. Her body lay slightly off to one side where the kitchen door had rolled her body and smeared the blood.

"Holy shit!" Gibson exclaimed, lifting Darlene's outer garment to reveal the wounds. "She must have been stabbed at least thirty, maybe forty times!"

"If you want, you can document the body, I'll get the kitchen, dining room, and living room. I don't think the bedroom is in play from what the district told us," Lang said.

As the two detectives feverishly scribbled their notes onto their tablets, the crime lab technician snapped frame after frame on the digital 35mm camera. Beginning with overall pictures of the apartment, the tech worked his way in through the front door and focused close on the body.

Finishing his task of documenting the dining room, Lang made his way into the living room where a small, gray, rectangular object lying on the floor, almost hidden beneath a dark-stained China cabinet, caught his attention.

"Hey, Gibson, take a look at this," Lang called out.

The two detectives hovered over the item and pondered the possibilities. The miniature digital recorder, lying face down, may have captured the murder. The detectives looked at each other knowing that the other was pondering the same thought. *Could it be that the recording device captured Darlene's last minutes on earth? And if so, did it even function after hitting the floor?* Then the detectives each considered the legal wrangling that loomed on the horizon later in a court proceeding. *Could it be that Darlene hit the record button just before her murder? What would be the legality of this find in court? Would the suspect have certain rights for this illegally obtained recording under Maryland State law?*

In recent days, the Clinton/Lewinski scandal raised legal scrutiny about Maryland's controversial wiretap laws after Linda Tripp secretly recorded conversations with Lewinski. Maryland wrestled in the national limelight with a controversial wiretap law that was now the number one story on every major news outlet. As a result, the 42nd President of the United States experienced an embarrassing impeachment and subsequent acquittal. Without a doubt, the two detectives knew the States Attorney's Office would have to mount an intense research effort to address this legal question.

"Hey Frank," Gibson called out to the crime lab technician, "I think we're going to want this."

****

Harold found a dark, quiet cul-de-sac just a few miles away to park his car and gather his thoughts. With the knifepoint resting against the hard console, Harold spun the knife in circles from its handle, much like a child playing with a spinning toy on a hardwood floor. Gazing into the unique patterns developed by the velocity of his rotating obsession, Harold became captivated in thought while watching the translucent figures dance before his eyes.

Upon seeing headlights approaching down the wooded road, Harold reclined his seat and laid back so the oncoming SUV wouldn't notice the occupied car. The headlights slowed on the main road and rounded the corner, giving all indications to Harold that the vehicle he wanted to avoid was heading straight for him. Harold wondered if the headlights belonged to a patrol car searching for him in his little, blue, Honda Civic hatchback.

Harold lay as still as he possibly could in his reclined position. It was hard not to move. He struggled to manage his breath since the confrontation in his mother's kitchen, fighting the urge to sit up, start the car and drive off. *If it's a cop, I'd never outrun him in this piece of shit,* he thought, while contemplating his options. *I'll have to do something; if he sees the tag, they'll know it's me for sure,* he further reasoned, trying to devise a plan.

As the headlights approached the Civic, the oncoming driver noted the strange vehicle in the neighborhood. *Strange,* she thought, as she approached the car. *Cars don't usually park along the street in our neighborhood.*

Realizing the unknown vehicle stopped next to his, Harold held his breath and closed his eyes, his brain frantically straining for an idea to ward off his potential capture. Listening intently, Harold waited to hear the sound of a car door shutting that would give him all certainty that someone would discover his whereabouts. However, as seconds turned into minutes, Harold heard nothing, except for the winding of the engine as the unknown car drove off. Sitting up in his seat, he carefully watched the SUV through his rear view mirror as it pulled into a concealed driveway located just behind where he parked. Waiting a moment more, Harold watched the slender woman get out of the Ford Excursion with a bag of groceries and walk into the house.

"Shit!" he yelled slamming his fist onto the dashboard. "She's probably got my tag number. Now what? Think, Harold. Think."

As Harold came up with a plan, his cell phone vibrated, startling him.

****

"Harold? This is Detective Yates with the police department... look Harold; I'd like to talk with you about this situation. Where are you?"

"Yeah, right, I tell you where I am and you lock me up," Harold said.

"Harold, Darlene is dead and we need to talk with you. I don't want anyone else getting hurt... can we meet somewhere?"

"You're bullshitting me! It's not worth it."

"Look, Harold. So you're having a bad day. I've been talking to your mom and she says you haven't been taking your medicine. This is something we can work through, Harold. I just need to talk to you. So where can we meet?" Yates asked.

Silence fell as Harold considered the offer.

"I'll meet... but it's only gonna be you—no other cops and don't bring your gun," Harold demanded.

"Harold, you know I can't do that – especially without my gun," Yates said with a small smile.

"Forget it then!" Harold said as he ended the phone call.

Yates looked down at his cell phone, checking the screen, confirming that Harold indeed ended the call, heightening the game.

****

Harold finally devised a plan. Abandoning the Honda Civic at the back of the cul-de-sac, he walked down the long, two-lane roadway lined with woods along both sides. Not only was it one of the most remote areas in the suburbs, it was a place of quiet and peace. Walking along the road's edge, he listened closely to the crickets chirping as the late night's autumn breeze chilled his bones. A flicker of light deep within the woods caused Harold to pause and gander between the trees to make out the source. Tree branches bending in the breeze, Harold first suspected that someone with a flashlight was walking through the woods, perhaps a K9 officer hot on his trail. Nevertheless, he stood motionless for several minutes and waited for the breeze to die down. He identified the light source: a back porch light to a residence he never knew existed on this desolate road. His fears relieved, Harold gave a small grin and continued walking down the road, clutching the bloodstained butcher knife in his hand.

He walked for nearly a mile before he saw a new set of headlights closing in on him, the only set of headlights he had seen all night since the curious onlooker stopped next to his car in the cul-de-sac. This time his simple plan came all too quick.

Harold carefully slid the sharp butcher knife down the back of his pants, concealing it under three layers of shirts. Hiding the knife without slicing himself, he removed his outer shirt and tossed it into the wood line of the forest. *No need looking like the description being broadcasted over the police radio.* Continuing his stride, Harold walked as naturally as possible, keeping his attention focused on the oncoming headlights. As the moonlight gleaned against the pale vehicle, he noticed the translucent profile of the light bar mounted on the vehicle's rooftop. Harold's fear heightened. Recalling the color scheme of the local police cruisers that transported him in a number of prior arrests, Harold's heart raced as he realized he was not prepared for this scenario.

As the Jeep closed the gap, Harold lowered his head, avoiding eye contact with the driver and glancing from the corner of his eye to inspect the Jeep as it passed him.

"Damn!" he snorted under his breath, confirming that the vehicle was, in fact, a marked police unit.

Maybe he'll just keep going, he thought, continuing his casual stride.

Harold then quickened his pace, looking for an avenue of escape into the woods. Being so close to the unexpected house made him realize the dogs at the residence were already barking, evidently noticing him sometime while he was concentrating on the approaching officer.

Looking to the other side of the street, Harold quickly deducted that it provided little if any options for escape. Being unfamiliar with this stretch of highway, coupled with his fear of foreign terrain, Harold concluded he would just keep walking along the road and hope his description didn't alarm the officer.

****

Stanley Muher already had a long day himself and found the drive home quite relaxing as he tuned into the local classical station playing Rachmaninov's Piano Concerto #2 in C Minor, Adagio Sostenuto. Having spent late nights at the office for the past week and a half in preparation for the civil litigation case that was occupying too much of his time, this attorney found the drive home soothing as the delicate ivory tones intermingled with the swelling orchestral strings. Rounding the corner and hitting the straightaway, Muher bore down on the accelerator, opening up his shimmering black BMW Z3 2.5i.

The irregular pattern of the oncoming headlights caught Muher's attention as he gently applied the brake, getting a better glimpse of the activity just ahead in the roadway. Muher allowed his convertible to edge up as far as possible, and noticed the headlights on the other vehicle belonged to the local police department. An officer, who just stepped from the vehicle, was approaching a wayward pedestrian. Curious at the police activity now unfolding in front of his two-seater sports car, Muher depressed the clutch and shifted the gear selector back to first gear as he waited for the road to clear.

Muher watched the officer walk halfway into the roadway between the police vehicle and the subject. It seemed just a little unusual that the officer had not activated his emergency lights, in order to give other travelers better warning of the temporary road obstruction. Nonetheless, as dark and desolate as the road was, who could miss the activity? Muher reached over and depressed the button, lowering his window to hear more about what was causing his delay.

"Show me your hands!" Muher heard the officer demand of the pedestrian.

The pedestrian raised his left hand while keeping his right in the small of his back. Muher became more intent on the scene unfolding just feet off his front bumper of his car. He gripped the steering wheel and leaned in to better view the events through the glare cast across his windshield by the officer's headlights.

"Sir! Show me your hands!" Muher heard the officer shout again, this time with more authority.

Cocking his eye at the strangeness of the non-compliant pedestrian, Muher gasped as he could now see the stranger sliding a large knife out from the small of his back.

Almost instinctively the officer positioned his hand up onto his service weapon, unsnapped the safety snaps, and firmly gripped the weapon's handle. As a deranged look filled the pedestrian's eyes, Muher's brain raced with ways that he could inform the officer that the suspect was extracting a knife, a large one at that. However, he was unable to coordinate any muscle movements that would permit him to yell a warning or to exit the vehicle and come to the officer's aid. No, the terror of the moment froze Muher to his plush leather seat as his body jerked and convulsed with uncoordinated movements that benefited no one. He would reach for the door handle to get out while his will pulled his arm back, causing the second arm to reach for the cellphone. Then his body would abandon its attempt to secure the cellphone as his hands now fidgeted with the gearshift selector. Not knowing what to do, Muher found that he could only sit, watch, and wait.

"I'm going to kill you!" Muher heard the pedestrian announce, raising the butcher knife over his head. Muher's body now froze rigid. He sucked in a deep breath and became pressed by an unknown force to witness the deadly encounter unfold.

The officer, who was nearly upon the suspect, raised his left hand in self-defense as he scampered backwards stumbling over his feet while rocking his pistol backwards to free it from its holster. With the pedestrian now nearly atop the officer, Muher watched the tide turn in complete amazement as the stumbling officer righted himself, established a level shooting platform, firmly gripped the pistol with both hands and unleashed three consecutive rounds at the advancing suspect.

For Muher, time stood still. The officer and pedestrian became frozen in time like two statuesque sculptures preserved forever, as three distinct flames could be seen along the darkened wood path.

The knife was the first to topple as it plummeted to the asphalt and tumbled far from the pedestrian's reach. The pedestrian took two staggering steps towards the officer, who was now backing up while maintaining the gun's sights square on his target.

The rounds knocked the wind and the fight out of the pedestrian who fell onto the pavement and peered up through the treetops into the starry night sky.

"3 Adam 14 dispatch… shots fired… shots fired… suspect is down." The officer's breath waned as the initial adrenalin rush now dissipated. "I need a medic to Piney Creek Mill Road," the officer yelled over the radio.

"3 Adam 14, I'm direct on the shots fired and the medic. Are you injured?"

"Negative dispatch… the medic is for the suspect."

****

Harold lay in the middle of the roadway feeling every corner of his body growing colder with each passing second. Glancing past his left shoulder, he could see the red stream of blood flowing from the severed femoral artery, parted just seconds earlier by one of the officer's hollow point rounds. Partly raising his hand towards the sky, Harold started mumbling.

"Hey! Buddy, I've got an ambulance on the way," the officer said reassuring his attacker.

"Won't matter," Harold replied in a faint voice. "What's done is done."

Harold's hand fell to his sides as his last breath escaped his lungs.

Seated motionless in his drivers seat, astonished at what he just witnessed, Muher lowered his head, offering a simple prayer of thanksgiving for the officer's safety and a prayer for the unfortunate soul, whom he believed, was now standing in the presence of God Almighty.

CHAPTER TWO

The gunpowder had barely finished dissipating from the air before the detectives realized, in spite of the enormous formalities in completing the mountainous paperwork and processing the few items of evidence to dispel any 'conspiracy theories,' the recent murder/suicide by cop investigation was now closed. After standing throughout the day by the remains of Darlene and Harold, who lay side by side at the morgue, Yates returned to his office, dropping into his chair, exhausted from standing on the hard ceramic-tiled floor while the doctors carved into the two stiffened cadavers.

"How'd it go?" Lang asked.

"Well, Darlene has forty-three stab wounds in her chest and Harold has three gunshot wounds. The groin shot severed the artery; he didn't stand a chance," said Yates. "Anything on the digital recorder?"

"I was just getting ready to check that," Gibson said as he pulled latex gloves over his hands and grabbed the evidence envelope. Pulling open the unsealed flap, Gibson carefully laid the envelope sideways with just enough of a slant that the Panasonic digital recorder slid out onto the solid wood conference table. The three detectives encircled the table to glare at the electronic device, wondering if somehow, by some freak chance, technology captured the murder.

12

Gibson bent over to get a closer look as he oriented himself with the device's features. Pressing the small menu button, the display listed the dates and times of the stored recordings. Crooking his thumb at a sharp angle, Gibson navigated the directional button as he scrolled down the list of recordings.

"Here it is," he said, raising his eyebrow with some amazement. "Looks like the voice activation was on and we have seventeen minutes of recording from yesterday evening." Depressing the play button, Gibson cranked up the volume before situating the recorder in the middle of the conference table. The three detectives, captivated by what they hoped to hear, pulled up chairs and sat silently huddled over the digital recorder.

The first few seconds emulated sounds that each of the detectives had heard before. There was a clambering, as if a body-wire were being activated on a willing informant who consented to derive criminal information from a target of interest. Clicking noises followed by muffled rumblings indicated the operator of the Panasonic digital recorder undoubtedly activated the device and concealed it somewhere on her person; most likely concealed loosely in her purse.

A female's voice followed the squeal of a screeching screen door opening.

"Harold? Harold? Where are you, you asshole?" the female barked.

Low clattering rumbles from a distance answered the female, but the words were inaudible.

"Where's my money?" the gruff female voice demanded.

"I ain't got your money!" answered the more faint male voice. "By the way, you owe *me* money."

"I don't owe you shit!" said the female.

"The hell you don't! You owe me $1,200 from all my smoke you lost!"

"My ass!" replied the female. "*You* lost *my* weed. I bought that shit and you were supposed to break it down into tens and sell it off. You probably smoked it all. Whatever you did with it, you owe *me* $1,200!"

The investigators looked up at each other, grinning as they tried to wrap their heads around the concept of a female drug dealer. With Yates and Lang having pulled stints in the district level detective unit that primarily focused on community drug complaints, both knew it was usually the guys who were carrying the product while armed with guns, while the girls tagged along for the ride, exchanging sexual favors for moments of temporary bliss. Focusing their attention back to the playing audio, the detectives listened as the argument continued.

"Look Harold, I want my money and I want it now."

"Well, you ain't getting it!"

"Yes, Harold! I'm getting my money and I'm getting it today, right now!"

"No, you're not!"

"Over my dead body," she replied, bringing a hush on the recording and in the homicide office as detectives realized how Darlene's words may have put the idea into Harold's head. The detectives knew it was only a matter of time before Harold's rain of violence would pour over Darlene.

"Harold? What the hell are you doing? Harold?" the female asked as clanging dishes echoed in the distant background.

"Oh, my God! Oh, my GOD! Harold! Put it down! Damn it! Don't do this! I didn't mean it," she cried out in sudden terror.

Shuffling noises heightened as each detective closed his eyes, remembering the layout of the apartment and the areas of evidentiary interest from processing the scene. They listened intently, hearing Darlene and Harold scuffling, knocking unknown items and bouncing off furniture as they clanged and thudded across the kitchen floor.

Darlene continued to plead with Harold to drop the knife. Without warning, the detectives heard a sudden thud that caused them to wince. Darlene's pleas suddenly stopped. The nauseating thumping noise was repeated over and over, no doubt, the detectives imagined in their own minds, the administration of the forty or so stab wounds they counted earlier that day.

"God forgive you, Harold. God forgive you for what you've done," Darlene mumbled as she gasped for air. Then, in a small whimpering voice, the detectives could hear Darlene's last words, gurgling through the blood laying in the back of her throat. "Help me get to heaven... please, God, help me get to heaven." The digital recorder fell awkwardly silent.

****

She leaned over and looked at the alarm clock that was setting atop the television tray, pulling double duty as a nightstand. The red neon lights displayed "2:23" across the darkened digital screen. *Please, just a few hours of sleep*, she thought as she listened to her colicky two-month-old daughter wrestle in the bassinet and begin a new regimen of screaming. Melissa threw back the covers and tugged on the overhead string, immediately illuminating the stark light bulb dangling from the floor joist in the cool, damp basement bedroom. Looking around the cluttered living space in her 'makeshift' room, Melissa found the canister of dry baby formula and the half-emptied bottle from the last feeding, not more than an hour ago.

Maybe she's wet, she wondered as she felt the inside of the diaper and found it to be dry. *She can't be hungry – I just fed her.* Melissa lifted the bottle and gave it a shake. *Wonder if I can nuke this?* she thought, looking to save as much money as possible on her limited income. *But, it might burn her mouth.* With a shrug of her shoulders, Melissa inverted the bottle and stuck the lukewarm nipple into Abigail's mouth without any further concern.

Born just two months earlier and weighing in at 5 pounds, 3 ounces, Abigail Spencer struggled to put on the necessary weight before coming home to the dreary living conditions so graciously provided by her grandparents. With the established homeowners enjoying the luxuries of their spacious bedroom in the main quarters of the upstairs, their misguided daughter, who was struggling to get by, found her place of abode in the dungeon below.

As Melissa manipulated a blanket and two small pillows to prop up the bottle, Abigail found initial relief in the formula offered to her. Like most colicky babies, Abigail quickly tired of the routine, spitting out the nipple, followed by a mouthful of formula, as she resumed her ear piercing wails. Flailing her tiny frail arms back and forth in a strange jerky motion, Abigail's legs mimicked her arms as they contorted irregularly, kicking the covers out from the bassinet, and dumping the bottle onto its side.

Melissa tearfully took in the moment, regretting the many decisions that forged her life and brought her to this empty despair. There must to be some way of erasing the memories, picking up the pieces, and starting over. A failed marriage with an unpredictable man she hardly knew was in and of itself more than enough for anyone to endure. Propelled into the doldrums of being a single parent was almost too much to bear. Life had not been easy, nor had it been fair. As life's dreams became disillusionments because of the reality of her present complexities, Melissa struggled to conquer the moment, quiet her baby, and desperately find some much-needed sleep.

An idea easily crept into her mind only two nights earlier when the crying episodes began, but, she never acted on it. Unsure of the affects on such a tiny person, she knew the calming sensation it had on her and decided that with a small careful dose, perhaps, just a drop may give her respite from the third sleepless night in a row.

Reaching for the bottle, Melissa pressed down firmly on the lid to twist open the childproof cap. Then, covering the small round opening with the tip of her finger, she inverted the bottle just enough to feel her skin moisten with the fluid. Being careful not to administer too much, Melissa found a spit rag hanging on the bassinet's side and wiped the excess off. With her left hand softly caressing Abigail's tiny frail head, she placed her dampened finger into her mouth and watched as her firstborn quietly closed her mouth around her finger. Instantly, with pure natural instinct, Abigail started sucking, pulling the fingertip to the roof of her mouth with a great deal of suction.

It was days since Melissa had seen her baby rest peacefully as Abigail lulled herself into a deep winter's sleep.

Melissa pulled her finger from the child's mouth, returned the dislodged blankets back into the bassinet, and covered her precious child before giving her a small peck on the cheek.

"Good night!" the mother said softly into her daughter's ear. "Sweat dreams..."

****

The aroma of fresh morning coffee drifted across the quaint country kitchen as it finished brewing, arousing Lang from his Saturday morning slumber. Pouring himself a fresh cup of joe, Lang carefully sipped the dark roast as his pager erupted, alerting him to the call for service.

"What do we have, Erickson?" Lang asked after calling into the communications center.

"Sounds like a SIDS death in the southwest district. Lieutenant Hughes is standing by at the scene."

****

"But I don't understand, Melissa, everything was quiet last night," the mother said to her stoic daughter.

"What do you mean it was quiet, mother?" came the indignant response. "She's was crying all night long. I haven't had any sleep in days!"

"What your mother means, honey, is that we didn't hear anything or know that you were having these problems with Abigail. Baby, you should have come to us and asked us for help."

"You couldn't see that I've been dragging my ass around here, not getting any sleep?" Melissa asked sarcastically.

"Easy now..." the uniform officer warned as the front door opened and the two homicide detectives entered the foyer and found their way to the assembled family in the formal living room.

Pleasantries were exchanged; hands shook with a warm

greeting, in spite of the awkwardness of the moment. The detectives found themselves seated comfortably on the chestnut brown Laramie sofa with Melissa and her parents adjacent from on another.

"Can you tell me a little bit about what happened last night?" Detective Thomas Cartwright asked the grieving mother.

"Well, for the past few days Abigail's been crying and hasn't been sleeping much, except during the day – she sleeps then! But at night, after I come home from work, she eats well and sleeps for about an hour starting at 8:00, but then she wakes up and starts fussing, usually into the early morning hours. She might fall back to sleep an hour or two before I have to get up and go to work."

"Is she colicky?" asked Cartwright.

"I guess – she just won't sleep," Melissa answered as she wiped the tears from her eyes.

"So what do you do when she doesn't sleep? Rock her? Feed her? Take her for a ride in the car?"

A ride in the car? That would have been a good idea. The suggestion of a car ride hadn't ever crossed her mind, but now that it was out in the open, she wished she had thought of it before taking the measures she had.

"I check to see if she's wet, then feed her," came the humble answer.

Cartwright jotted down the few notes into his notepad, and then looked off towards the curio cabinet for a moment as he formulated his next series of questions.

"Mr. and Mrs. Spence, part of what we need to do is search the house for the purpose of the investigation. We need to look around and inspect the living conditions, the bedroom, and the area where Abigail died. You have two options at this point. The first requires us to get a search warrant, which wouldn't be a problem in this case. We would simply maintain custody of the house while I go and write up an application, then I'd go see a judge who would review it, and given the circumstances in this case, would sign the search warrant. The second option would be to have you provide us with consent to search. Because the house is yours and Melissa doesn't rent from you, all that would be required is filling out the form, and getting your signature. At that point we could search the house, document the scene, and be out of here in about an hour or two."

Mr. Spence leaned his elbows in to his knees. "Detective, I'll sign the consent so that my family doesn't have to endure this any longer than necessary."

"That'll be fine," Cartwright said pulling out the form.

****

Cartwright opened the door leading to the musty cool basement. Sliding his hand along the darkened wall, he found the light switch that illuminated two fluorescent shop lights suspended at two different ends of the basement. Descending the battleship-gray wooden stairway, the detectives found themselves sandwiched amongst a cluster of lifelong dreams and memories stowed away from another era.

"The bedroom's back here," Cartwright said to Lang as they navigated through the piles of boxes nearly reaching the ceiling.

The room, dark just by the nature of its location and the blanket that hung in the doorway keeping out the artificial light streaming from the fluorescent lamps, was cool and dank. Cartwright and Lang extracted miniature maglights giving temporary light for them to struggle their way through the cluttered bedroom.

Pulling on the chain of the rudimentary light fixture nailed above, the detectives found themselves standing in a cramped room that offered neither the comfort, nor luxuries that the upstairs living room afforded moments earlier.

Surveying the tiny living space, Cartwright wondered how anyone, especially a new mother, could have effectively functioned in this room. Before long, the foul stench lingering in the room pressed against the two investigators. A pile of soiled baby diapers in the corner trashcan in conjunction with seven or eight partially filled baby bottles containing soured formula all added to the discomfort of the room. With the queen-size bed pushed into the far corner and the nightstand pinched into the opposite corner, the bureau and bassinet took what remained of the narrow walking space. Even so, piles of clothes needing laundered and those already through the process, sat strewn in mismatched piles across the bed, floor, and bureau. With the occupants fighting for use of every inch of space in the room, it came as no surprise to the detectives when they observed that the mother had stowed Abigail's clean laundry and spit rags right in the bassinet.

With the ambulance having already transported Abigail's rigid little body to the Johns Hopkins Emergency Room hours before in a vain attempt to give her one last chance at life, the investigators determined the brunt of their work would come by way of the autopsy room.

"You know Tom," Lang said searching the bureau drawers, "these cases usually end up being a 'shaken baby' death, and Mom ends up getting charged with manslaughter."

"One thing's for sure," Cartwright said, "if that's the case, we'll find out for certain later this morning at the autopsy when they crack open her skull."

"We might want to lock Mom into a story before all of that becomes known."

Cartwright immediately abandoned the area he was searching and returned upstairs, pulling Melissa off to the side to speak with her in a more private setting. Seating themselves at the small, wooden kitchen table, Melissa poured Cartwright a cup of coffee before retrieving her own and taking her seat across the table.

"Melissa, there are some preliminary and generic questions I need to ask you to better help the doctor who'll be performing the autopsy. I can assure you these questions are typical and standard in investigations such as this one. I'm not in any way pointing any fingers at you to say that something inappropriate happened."

"I understand, you're just doing your job," Melissa said with resignation.

"Melissa, sometimes when a baby gets colicky, like Abigail

did, the parents get pretty frustrated. I have to ask, did you get frustrated?"

"Yeah, quite a bit! My husband left me when he found out I was pregnant again. We already have a 12-year-old girl who just started high school. We didn't use protection one night and the next thing you know, I'm pregnant," Melissa explained staring at her wavering reflection in her steaming mug. Unable to draw her undivided attention and making direct eye contact with Detective Cartwright, Melissa continued. "He left me for some stripper down from the Block. She might make a lot of money, but that bitch will never be any good for him." Giving a small wry smile and raising an eyebrow, Melissa reflected on her life for a moment, telling Cartwright her story.

"You know, Abigail's a crack baby!" she said looking for the first time at Cartwright to measure his reaction. "I had a little problem getting my life straight," she explained while reaching for a cigarette and lighter conveniently waiting for her across the table. Drawing out a Marlboro, Melissa pinched the cigarette between her lips, lit the end, and drew in a long, hard drag as she waited to see if the detective would pass judgment on her as many of her family members already had.

"You know," she continued "I used to sell my ass to get my heroin fixes."

Sensing the moment, Cartwright looked at Melissa with a fatherly look and spoke the best advice he could give her. "Melissa, we all make mistakes; none of us, not one, is perfect. So you've made some mistakes in your life. Looks like you have good parents who are genuinely concerned about you and want to see you become the woman they always hoped you to be. You just need a little help. We all need a little help now and then."

Melissa looked at Cartwright rather stunned at the possibility that she could even achieve becoming a woman of integrity as her parents hoped. "I don't know, Detective; for some of us, that's hard to accomplish."

"Well, there's no doubt that you've been pretty frustrated – trying to get your life on track with a newborn baby to boot. But I need to ask you, were you alone with Abigail all night last night?"

"In the basement? Yeah. My parents sleep upstairs; they never came down last night; or any other night for that matter."

"And did you have anyone staying with you in the basement last night—new boyfriends, old boyfriends, estranged husbands?" Cartwright asked with a crooked grin.

"Nope, it was just me and Abby."

"From talking with the officers when we arrived, it sounds like Abby finally settled down for you around 2:00 in the morning, and then you found her at..."

"6:30... I found her dead at 6:30," Melissa said, finishing the detective's thought as she stared with glassed over eyes.

"Other than her formula, is Abby on any medication?"

"No."

"So you didn't give her anything last night to settle her down."

"No... nothing!"

"This is really important, Melissa. At any point in time last night, or even over the past several days, did you shake Abby, trying to get her to settle down?" Cartwright asked.

"No, I just checked her diaper and gave her some formula. She *finally* settled down, and I *finally* went to bed."

"Would you mind writing that down in a statement?" Cartwright asked, offering her the official statement form.

****

As Cartwright extrapolated the necessary information from Melissa, Lang's prying eyes continued searching the basement bedroom for any signs of irregularities. A thorough search of the bureau and nightstand drawers did not yield the typical drug stash that Lang routinely found when he was a younger detective working the local precinct drug unit. They did, however, reveal a great deal of tattered and torn notices from Johns Hopkins, diagnosing Abigail with her addiction. Having examined each of the boxes in the room and verifying that each contained what the label indicated; Lang finished examining the bedroom with an unsettled feeling looming over him.

Stepping out from the bedroom, Lang looked around the remainder of the basement that still required searching. The task seemed immense. With a cursory look, Lang deducted that the upstairs occupants packed much of their belongings and stowed them on the opposite side of the basement. However, a small portion of the basement, where a changing table and metal shelving unit stood just outside Melissa's improvised bedroom door, needed searching.

Going through the changing table, Lang found the typical diapers, lotions, ointments, and baby powder neatly arranged awaiting the next diaper change. Lang shifted his attention to the metal shelving unit. In a rather organized and systematic way it bore items that Melissa found necessary for beginning her journey of this new life. Baby formula cans of all varieties were neatly stacked according to type and size. Clean bottles were uniformly arranged next to a small microwave residing on the second shelf up from the floor.

Additional baby lotions, ointments, and powders took up the middle shelves next to the vitamins and medications. Lang slowed his search, focusing on each bottle, lifting it up and reading the labels to explore what could possibly be contained within. Lifting the first bottle, the detective examined the label and verified its contents of vitamins. Making the note in his notepad, he replaced the pill bottle and moved to the next one. Turning it around, he was able to see Melissa's name properly printed across the label issued by the pharmacy from the Johns Hopkins Hospital. Unfamiliar with the labeling and style of medicine bottle, Lang carefully examined the label. His eyes opened wide upon seeing the medication's nomenclature.

What is that doing here?

CHAPTER THREE

The day was long, catapulting her evening schedule into a state of topsy-turvy, missing the children's dance practice *again* in order to make some headway in the settlement case that was slated for court the following Tuesday. As she climbed into her pearl white Cadillac Escalade SUV and opened the sunroof to enjoy the invigorating night air, she thought about how inflexible her client had been and how many evenings this legal entanglement kept her away from her husband and children. Tonight, she thought, would be a relaxing night; perhaps a light dinner, some white wine, a Riesling from the local vineyard, and her favorite book would help her to unwind from the day's stressful events.

Pulling into her driveway surrounded by the immaculate landscaping encircling the two-story brick estate, Jessica Henley eased her SUV into the three-car garage.

Funny, the timer on the lights aren't working again; the lights aren't on.

Placing the gearshift into park, Jessica looked over to the next spot in the garage and noticed that her husband's Jaguar was not home. With a quick glance at the dashboard clock, she noted that it was only 8:20 p.m. Her husband and two daughters should be home any minute from dance class. *Another late night.* Grabbing her purse, she made her way to the

24

door.

Stopping to fish out her house keys in the darkened garage, Jessica was startled to find as she went to place the key into the lock, the door sat slightly ajar and easily pushed open.

That's weird. Usually Mya keeps the doors closed and locked.

Dismissing her concern, Jessica pushed the door open, stepped into the kitchen, and settled her purse and keys on the edge of the island. Reaching for the light switch, she flicked the switch, finding the lights unresponsive.

"Damn it! What's going on?" she exclaimed while stamping her foot.

Trying each switch lined along the wall, Jessica realized the electric in the neighborhood must be out. She walked over to the kitchen window and gazed out across the meadow to the Simmons' house down by the stream. *Their lights are on.* Her curiosity heightening, Jessica rummaged through the kitchen junk drawer, found the flashlight, and tested the device. *Well, that works* she thought as she flipped the switch, casting a dull light back towards the garage. *If I can find the circuit breaker, maybe I can figure out what's going on.*

As Jessica made her way back out to the garage, she jumped when the center garage door jolted opened automatically. Frozen by her fear, she watched the door creep upwards as light poured into the garage, now blinding her. As the intense light flooded the garage interior, she heard the car doors unlatch.

"Mommy" cried her two girls simultaneously as they came running towards her in their matching leotards. "We missed you at practice," the older of the two said.

"Hi, honey," John Hensley said shutting the driver's door, his jacket folded over his arm. "What's going on with the lights?"

Exhaling a deep breath, Jessica gave her husband a grin. "I don't know, honey, I was just coming out to check on that."

"Where's Mya?" asked John about the family's housekeeper.

John turned towards the dark corner of the garage navigating his way past the bicycles and mowers with the dim flashlight. *We really need to get a brighter flashlight,* he thought as his foot became entangled in an orange extension cord, nearly sweeping him off of his feet.

Opening the panel door, John saw that the main circuit breaker had indeed tripped.

"Ah, here's the problem," he announced. "The breaker tripped."

"So why did the garage door open?" Jessica asked recalling her moment of fear.

"There's a battery back-up that kicks in whenever the electric goes out," John answered.

As John flipped the switch, the lights illuminated and life appeared to be normal once again. John inspected the electrical box and noticed that one of the other breakers immediately tripped again. *That's strange, wonder what's going on there?* John conferred with the panel guide to see what portion of the house breaker 23 controlled. *The maid's quarters, I'd better go up and see what's going on in Mya's apartment.*

****

For Mya, it was a chance of a lifetime that allowed her to immigrate into the United States some seven years ago. Born and raised in the depressed country of Burma in 1957, Mya's parents sold her into the sex-slave trade as a young woman to help meet the family's financial needs. The extra income helped ease the demand of feeding so many mouths. As she grew too old to be profitable in her 'trade,' Mya escaped her nightmare, and found work cleaning the residence of a prominent Burmese businessman who had strong business connections in America and secrets to hide. It was through this exquisite business relationship that Mya received her opportunity to travel to America on a work visa and make a go at living in the "land of the free and home of the brave." With her door of opportunity standing wide open, Mya took a step of faith, and sought out her new life in the rolling countryside of Maryland.

With experience in house cleaning, Mya found employment cleaning a prominent surgeon's house in the rural area of the county. When her visa expired, her employment ended. Mya found herself back in the deprivations of Burma longing to return to the States. With a little help from her Burma contact, Mya made application for citizenship and moved back to the northern hills of Maryland. This time she intended to stay. Her former employer found another housekeeper while she was in Burma, so Mya was referred to the Henley family, two salient civil attorneys specializing in medical malpractice suits.

When she unpacked her suitcase, Mya realized she finally had the world in her hand: a luxurious apartment in a spacious mansion estate overlooking a 500-acre horse farm, Mya found a place of comfort and rest and was even able to begin learning a little of the English language thanks to her mid-day soap opera respites.

****

John opened the door and climbed the back stairwell leading to the guest apartment. As he neared the top landing, he instinctively gave a huff to the unpleasant odor of burnt plastic and wiring lingering about.

"Mya? My-ya?" he called out into the darkness.

The utter silence left him feeling out of sorts as he fished out the flashlight stashed in his back right pocket. Flipping the switch, John felt powerless as the darkness swallowed up the dim light in the vast depths of the room. With a great deal of precision, he started searching from the corner of the room near the kitchen where he figured the electrical failure may have originated. Scanning the counter tops, he noticed no appliances plugged into any of the ground fault switches; the receptacles all appeared normal. John continued down the long wall towards the television set noting nothing irregular there either. As he glanced up towards the bedroom that embodied a magnificent view of the lush green pastures, John saw a heap lying on the bed beneath the window. Drawing near, the overwhelming smell of stagnant blood consumed him as he gazed upon his nearly decapitated housemaid lying in her blood-soaked bed.

****

"We thought we should call you boys out to this one," the uniformed sergeant said to the detectives arriving in the driveway.

"So, what's one of these places going for? Say 1.5, maybe 2 million?" Lang said walking up to the huddled group of detectives.

"Two million, easy," Corporal Mariano Davis answered. "I was thinking about buying a place up here when I get promoted to sergeant," he jested.

"You've got to be smart enough to pass the test first, Marc!" Lang whipped back.

"Hey, I got this far," Davis said.

"Yeah, one rank, I wouldn't be bragging just quite yet. What do we have?" Lang asked.

Officer Wisniewski stepped up with his spiral bound notebook, flipping his pages backwards to the start of his notebook. "Mr. and Mrs. Henley are attorneys downtown for a large firm. They came home this evening and found their housemaid, a Burmese immigrant, lying on her bed with a circular electric saw cut deep into her throat—her head's nearly off!" the officer exclaimed, shaking his head in shocked disbelief.

"Okay, so does it look like a murder? Or is this a suicide?" Davis asked the uniformed officers.

"Beats the hell out of us. That's why we called you all out. I'm not saying it's one thing and then having it turn up to be something else – no, I'm not putting my ass out there like that," the sergeant replied.

"Guess that's why they pay us the big bucks! Right, Corp?" Lang asked Davis.

"We ought to go in and see what we got," Davis said.

"You might want to put these on," Officer Wisniewski said, dangling a pair of protective booties in front of the detective's faces.

"Is it that bad in there?" Davis asked.

"Yeah, And we don't want to mess up those fancy Bostonian shoes you're all wearing, now do we? Oh, by the way, we unplugged the saw—the breaker kept tripping."

The inquisitive entourage meandered through the downstairs living room, into the kitchen, and up the back servant's stairwell into the apartment.

"Holy shit!" Davis blurted. "The apartment alone is bigger than my entire house!"

Walking through the living area, everything appeared in its place; nothing amiss, nothing missing. The living quarters were immaculate, all except for the bedroom floor, which was drenched with a frothy, bright red puddle of blood. Mya's stone cold eyes were glaring off to the distant corner, looking away from the still steaming skill saw. Her right hand laid face up as if reaching out for help at her very last moment.

"It's rather oxymoronic!" said Davis.

"What's that?" asked Lang.

"She looks so peaceful lying there but look at how she died."

The analogy hit right on point. Mya appeared to have found a peace that she never experienced before. But the manner in which death transported her to this new peaceful life remained to be determined. Was it self-inflicted or did she die at the hand of another?

"Well, Detective," Davis said, "Is this a suicide or murder?"

The detective's eyes perused the scene, looking for one clear, decisive clue that would confirm murder or suicide, but nothing relevant confirmed to the investigators one way or the other. Mya's story of immigrating to the United States and now working in a luxurious multimillion-dollar estate for two renowned attorneys inclined one to suspect that Mya had died at the hands of another. Then, as the detectives closely looked at the physical evidence surrounding them at the scene, they suspected the unfathomable.

"Look," Lang announced pointing to the saw's electric cord. "All of the connections, into the wall and here at the extension cord; they're all freshly taped up with some electrical tape like someone didn't want it to come unplugged accidentally!"

Davis perused the area surrounding the bed. "Here you go," he said discovering the small half used roll of electrical tape lying on a nearby bookshelf.

"And look at the blood spray! There's a ton of it! Blowing back this way, if she was killed, the killer could have only been standing right here to cut her throat. He would have been drenched in blood, tracking it across the floor and there's no indication from the blood pattern that something, or someone, was standing here to block the spray against the wall."

"Okay, so you're saying that she killed herself with a skill saw?" the officer asked.

"Pretty much! We know this: nobody else cut her throat, and based on the amount of blood that's laying here, she bled for awhile."

"Damn, man! You mean she felt it?" asked the officer.

"I don't know. She may have gone unconscious, but her heart was beating for some time to pump all this blood out before she died," answered Lang.

"All right, so tell me this—what's the deal with the electric going out?" asked the sergeant.

Lang took his flashlight and illuminated the saw's blade lodged deep into Mya's neck.

"You see that white part back there?" Lang asked.

"Yep!" the sergeant answered.

"That's her vertebrae—bone. I'm not sure how sharp this blade is, but they use special blades downtown to open your skull to get your brain out during the autopsy. My bet is the blade wasn't sharp enough and bound up on the bone. After awhile something's got to give."

"So, the circuit breaker trips," the sergeant said, reaffirming the lesson learned.

"Yep! The medical examiner will be able to better see tomorrow morning during the autopsy," Lang confirmed.

Having lost interest in the unique selection of death, Davis wandered back across the studio apartment and inspected Mya's writing desk where she often sat and wrote letters back home to a handful of friends in Burma.

"Did you all see this envelope on the desk?" Davis asked.

"No, who is it addressed to?" asked Officer Wisniewski.

"No one. The front is blank, but it's got a hand written note inside."

Pulling a fresh pair of latex gloves from his left jacket pocket, Davis draped the purple gloves around his hands and emptied the contents onto the writing table. Sorting through the three handwritten pages he quickly discerned that the pages were handwritten in some form of an Asia language, undoubtedly Burmese.

"I wonder if it's a suicide note," Davis expressed loudly.

"Could be; we could have crime lab take it and then send a copy over to the FBI for a translation," Lang suggested.

"Absolutely, I'm gonna get the ME's office started out this way," Davis said flipping open his cell phone.

****

With the squad finishing its ritual sushi dinner around the conference table, the detectives and supervisors each found their way back to their respective dimly-lit desks. Each would pour through the pile of paperwork as they looked to finish the remaining hours of the three to eleven shift.

Lang skimmed through the recent pile of manila envelopes dumped onto the far corner of his desk and the one with "OFFICE OF THE CHIEF MEDICAL EXAMINER" stamped in the upper left hand corner grabbed his eye. He opened the envelope and immediately recognized the contents as the official police copy of an autopsy report. Sliding the report out onto his desk, the name "Abigail Spencer" appeared in the appropriate name block. Reclining back for a brief moment, Lang slowly read through the medical jargon noting that much of the report accounted for the normalcy of the various measured levels of the human body's composition.

Lang flipped the page again and started reviewing the intoxication levels recorded through the multitude of blood screenings calculated in the laboratory in the weeks prior to the generation of the report.

"That's good—that's good—uh oh," Lang said quietly in his chair as he saw the elevated numbers under the fifth category. Turning to the next page to review the more detailed breakdown of the intoxication summary, Lang's eyes bulged when he read the details of the report.

"Cartwright!" Lang yelled out the office door to the detective who just stepped out to the kitchenette to freshen up his mug of coffee. "Better get in here! You've got a murder!"

****

Cartwright was ending his telephone call as Lang returned to the office with Melissa Spencer who seemed lost and bewildered and stepped into an interview room at police headquarters.

"Melissa, have a seat right here. We'll be right back. Would you like anything to drink?" asked Cartwright.

Melissa shook her head, and then rubbed her arms to fight off the chill in the air.

Lang poured a hot cup of coffee and retreated to the back corner room where he flipped on the monitor and insured that the conversation about to unfold would be forever memorialized in digital format. With "REC" flashing on the screen, Lang plugged in the headset and sat back on the sofa awaiting the outcome.

****

"Melissa, do you know why you're here?" asked Cartwright.

"I would suppose that it has something to do with Abigail's death. Has the medical examiner made a determination?"

"Melissa, do you remember our discussion that morning at the house when you found Abigail dead in her bassinet?"

"Vaguely. It's so blurry now," she answered, trying to figure out where the detective was taking her.

It was prudent, Melissa thought, to be extremely cautious at this juncture of the investigation. Everything seemed to be moving in the right direction for her, finally, and by making one foul mistake could up dump the entire apple cart. *Be careful with your answers.*

"Melissa, we spoke at great lengths about what had happened throughout the course of the night with Abigail. We talked about times you changed her diaper, times you fed her, and times you administered medication. Remember?"

"Like I said, it's all blurry."

"Well, Melissa, let's go over it again. Tell me about your last night with Abigail."

Melissa's eye's lifted up and darted directly into the detective's. *How dare you challenge me!* she thought in anger, seething at the possibility that her life could potentially be derailed yet one more time.

"It's like I said. She wouldn't go to sleep, so I checked her diaper and she was dry, I fed her more formula, but she seemed full. Finally, around 2:00 in the morning, she started to doze off and I was able to get some sleep," answered Melissa gritting her teeth.

"Did you give Abigail anything?" the detective asked pointedly.

"No!"

"Are you sure?"

"Yes!"

"Melissa, it's really important that you try to remember if you gave Abigail anything—*anything* that night," Cartwright pleaded with her not wanting to believe that a mother would intentionally kill her child.

"Damn it! I've told you a hundred times that I didn't give Abigail anything that night!" Melissa yelled, tears now streaming down her face.

"What about methadone?" asked the detective finally laying down his hand.

Silence fell in the room as Melissa sat back in her chair, turned her head away from Cartwright, and wiped the tears from her cheek to recompose herself.

"I told you Detective Cartwright, I didn't give Abigail anything," she said calmly, keeping her emotion in check.

"And you were alone with her all night?"

"Yes," her answer absolute.

Wrenching his face into a stern look, Cartwright addressed his suspect. "Melissa, the autopsy report came back from the medical examiner's office. Everything checks normal regarding Abigail's toxicity," Cartwright said.

Melissa sat back, her head falling back as a grin grew upon her face announcing the much-needed relief that she longed to experience since that morning. Drawing in a deep breath, Melissa exhaled, purging her worry and fear.

"Everything came back clean—except for one level," Cartwright said.

As quickly as relief washed over her, Melissa found herself glaring at the detective with a new and genuine concern.

"Melissa, Abigail tested positive for the presence of methadone—"

"That's impossible," Melissa said cutting off the detective. "There's no way that…"

"Actually Melissa, there is. We know that you're on the methadone program at the hospital and that they've started a new program, allowing you to self-medicate at home. You simply fill the prescription and give yourself the medication when needed. But because of your addiction to heroin, Abigail was born an addict. Melissa, Abigail wasn't colicky, she was in withdrawal, and you knew it. So you thought that if you gave her a little dab of methadone, her craving would be satisfied, and she would sleep, didn't you?"

The question came without a response. These questions usually remained unanswered once the detectives figured out what had happened. They were able to flawlessly convey the story back to the suspect as if they were in the room during the murder.

"She went to sleep and never woke up again—that's because for an infant her size, any amount, even a drop, is a lethal dose."

Melissa sat quietly, taking every word in, unable to control the tears that rushed down her face.

"Melissa, your own words convicted you today."

34

"Convicted? Wait a minute! What do you mean *convicted?*" she asked in her horror.

"Melissa, it wasn't what you said, it's what you didn't say. If we had the truth right from the beginning, we wouldn't be here today. You didn't, so you're being charged with first degree murder."

Melissa's mouth fell, gaping uncontrollably. No words formed as Cartwright pulled the handcuffs from his belt and secured her to the pole in the interview room. Stunned and amazed at the development, Melissa could find no appropriate reaction to her legal predicament.

Detective Lang sat a moment longer on the couch in the monitoring room as Cartwright left, and pulled the door shut, leaving Melissa in complete solitude. Lang watched her on the monitor as she looked around the room rather nervously, and then tried jerking her right hand free from her chains. The reality of the moment sunk in. Within a few moments, Melissa found a measure of peace as she leaned over onto the table, cupped her free arm around her face and fell asleep.

CHAPTER FOUR

The mood proved quite festive as the crowd of once familiar acquaintances assembled around the bar at Bill Bateman's restaurant at the north end of town. Only five years had passed since many of them had seen each other on the occasion of the Class of 2001's graduation from Central High. As the crowd grew larger, hugs, smiles, and beer sloshing toasts filled the joyous atmosphere.

Stacey circled the crowd, finding a small, narrow opening allowing her to lean into get the bartender's attention.

"What'll you have Miss?" the bartender asked, wiping down a clean glass.

"Another Coors Light, please," she said, tilting her head with an innocent smile.

Her voice caused Calvin to turn and see his old high school crush standing there patiently waiting for the frosted mug to fill with her favorite ale.

"Stacey?" he asked.

"Calvin!" Stacey replied with some surprise. "I didn't think I was going to see you here. I thought you enlisted."

"Didn't work out," he explained. "They medically discharged me—bum leg from high school football," he said, shrugging his shoulders. "How about you? Where did you end up going after high school?"

"Maryland University at College Park. I'll be finishing my business undergraduate program this year and going into the MBA program, next," she said with a great deal of enthusiasm for her accomplishment. "Any idea what kind of business you'd like to get into?"

"No, haven't decided on that, yet. I thought I'd wait to see where fate took me."

Stacey's order came without any further delay. She grabbed her frothing ale off the bar and turned towards her cluster of friends who had commandeered a nearby table with a group of high-back stools.

"So, Stacey, now that I'm back in town, could I get your phone number?" Calvin asked with some anticipation.

"Sure!" she replied as she retrieved her cell phone from her back pants pocket while perfectly balancing her beer in the other. She thumbed open the flip phone and dialed in Calvin's cell phone number that he anxiously rattled off at her request. Pressing the send button, it only took a second until Calvin felt his phone vibrating on his belt holster and retrieved his phone.

"Now you have my number," she said before closing her phone, offering a delicate smile, and turning her attention back towards her waiting friends.

Calvin's eyes became transfixed as he watched Stacey saunter back to her friends who hadn't noticed the impromptu conversation. Calvin was unable to break his eyes away from her; the once boney, stringy-haired blonde was now a drop-dead gorgeous bombshell. With his gaze transfixed on his new love, Calvin walked back towards his group and commented on how much of a crush he had had on Stacey while they were in high school. After seeing what a beautiful woman Stacey had grown and matured into, Calvin calculated his next move.

She's absolutely beautiful. His stare glued on her lovely, contoured form. *I've got to have her!*

****

The party raged well into the night before segregated fractions trailed off in opposing directions. Stacey decided she had enjoyed the company of her old girlfriends long enough and wanted to drop by Austin's house, see what was going on and maybe even stay the night. *Austin would certainly enjoy that!*

Finding street-side parking in front of the house this late at night was always a challenge, usually ending with her parking near the Unite Methodist Church at the far end of the street. With the exception of the Sunday morning and mid-week services, parking was usually available, and the walk was not too terribly far and was invigorating. As expected, Stacey found an available parking spot, this one a little closer to the house than usual. *That'll be good this late at night*, she thought as she parked the car, clicked the lock button on the remote and started her brisk trek down the sidewalk. Tossing her keys into her purse, Stacey heard the familiar Caribbean steel drum ringtone muffled in her back pocket. She recently came to love the tune, as corny as it sounded because it reminded her of her impending wedding to Austin and the Caribbean cruise they booked for their honeymoon.

At first glance, she did not recognize the phone number displayed on the caller ID. Then it clicked in just a few seconds: she remembered her conversation with Calvin earlier that night and the current phone number exchange that occurred. *I wonder what he wants this late at night?*

"Hello?"

"Stacey? It's Calvin. How are you?" His heart half stopped upon hearing her soft meek voice.

"I'm fine. What's up?" she asked, still inquisitive about the purpose of his call at this late hour.

"Listen, I was wondering, could we get together this evening and catch up on lost time?"

"Calvin, don't you think it's a little late at night to call?" she asked.

"It's only 12:45, and I was hoping that we could go out for some drinks, maybe even get a bite to eat over at the diner."

Not connecting Calvin's intentions, Stacey simply rebuffed the invitation, wanting to just get into the house and curl up with Austin on the ratty old futon couch. "Sorry, Calvin, We'll have to catch up with each other another time, I'm tied up the rest of the evening."

"Sure—I understand," he stuttered as disappointment sank deep into his chest. "Maybe we can get together another night this week."

"We'll see. I've got a pretty busy week ahead of me."

Not being very keen on the suggestion, Stacey simply ended the call with a quick goodbye. She flipped the phone closed and stuffed it back into her pocket as she walked in through the front door. Instinctively knowing that she would be coming in, Austin greeted his fiancée with a quick peck on the cheek and closed the front door.

"How'd it go?"

"The reunion was great! Susan, Rachel, and Tammi were all there! I was so excited they could make it."

"Well, come on in. I rented a movie—you interested?"

"Sure!"

After Stacey shed her coat and purse, the two nestled onto an oversized beanbag lying in front of the flat-screen television. As they fell into each other's embrace, Stacey's cell phone rang. Looking at the caller id, this time she immediately recognized the number, showing a little annoyance with a roll of her eyes.

"Calvin?" she asked answering the phone.

"Stacey! Oh good, you haven't gone to bed yet. I was really hoping that we could get together *tonight* and—"

"Calvin! I really don't appreciate you calling me so late, and I—"

"Yeah, but Stacey, I wanted to ask you out to dinner tomorrow night." He was able to eek in the question, catching her completely off guard.

"You're asking me out?" she clarified.

"Yeah."

Suddenly, it all made sense. "Look, Calvin, I'm engaged."

"Well, why did you give me your phone number then?" he asked, his tone becoming sharp and indignant.

"Because you said you wanted to catch up on old times. You didn't say anything about wanting to ask me out or I wouldn't have given you my number!"

"Whatever!" he said, slamming his phone closed, severing

the call.

Stacey sat amazed, staring at her display screen, trying to reason what had just happened.

"Who was that?" Austin asked with a crooked eyebrow.

"An old classmate, Calvin. He used to have a huge crush on me in high school."

"Calvin? Calvin Meadows? The puny, washed out, second-string running back from high school?"

"Yep, that's him," she said.

"He thinks you see something in *him*?" he asked.

"He shouldn't—"

Her cell phone begin ringing again, displaying the annoying phone number that was now beginning to plague her. Austin pulled the phone from her hand, glanced at the number, and then answered the call.

"Hello? Hello?" Austin said, finally prompting the caller to respond.

"Is Stacey there?"

"No jackass! This is her fiancée. Is there something I can help you with?"

Austin remembered the scrawny Calvin Meadows from his high school football days. Lean, thin, not very tall, Calvin barely made the cut to the team and Austin knew that with his six-foot four-inch brawny stature he could handle Meadows in a matter of seconds.

"Look asshole, quit calling my girl. In fact, it might be a good idea if you lost her number."

"Hey! How'd a girl like that get stuck with an asshole like you?" Calvin posed.

"Well, why don't you come over and find out," Austin retorted.

"No problem, bitch. Where do you live?"

Calling his bluff, Austin provided Calvin with his home address and clear directions. He was convinced that the scrawny sap would not show his face. Furthermore, he was not about to let anyone, especially little Calvin Meadows, harass his girl and speak to her the way that he had.

"Why did you give him your address?" Stacey asked,

backhanding Austin against his chest.

"He ain't coming over here! He's too scared. Come on, let's watch the movie."

****

Calvin threw the phone down in complete disgust.

"Randy, get your shit. We're going over to the east side tonight."

****

Austin and Stacey found themselves trying to focus on the movie while lost in their own individual thoughts about the unusual set of events that tainted their evening with ill emotions and quenched any chances of getting lost between the sheets. *This didn't go as expected.*

"You just want to go to bed?" Austin asked, noticing Stacey staring off into the corner of the room.

"I can't believe he was trying to ask me out," she said. "He was a jerk in high school, and he's still a jerk."

Austin offered a cordial smile, which immediately washed off his face when Stacey's phone rang once again. This time, Austin snatched the phone from Stacey's grasp and verified Calvin's number.

"Will you give it up?" Austin said in a stern voice.

"I'm out front, bitch. Come out and take care of me," Calvin said before hanging up the phone.

Austin immediately grabbed a sock and fished two balls, the eight ball and the cue ball, out of the corner pocket from the pool table. Dropping the balls into the sock, he felt confident that he armed himself with a modern day flail he could use to crack Calvin's head open if necessary.

"Austin! Where are you going?" Stacey cried out as he made his way to the door.

"I'm going to settle this once and for all," Austin said as he bolted out the front door and down the concrete steps.

Austin looked at the cars immediately parked in front of his house. They were all familiar, none occupied. It was then that glaring headlights down the roadway caught his eye. Stopped in the road near the Methodist church, Austin noticed the only thing moving on his street in the early morning hours. Tucking the homemade flail into his right front pocket, he made his way towards the unknown vehicle. The glaring lights prevented him from seeing who and how many were in the vehicle. He decided he better make sure the numbers were fair before deciding to get entangled into a brawl where he would be outnumbered and overtaken. *Be careful, Austin* he thought as he cautiously walked up the sidewalk through the dark looming shadows. *Watch yourself.*

Stacey could not bear to walk up the road with him, and elected to conceal herself in the darkened corner of the porch. From just behind a tall bush that provided some sense of cover and ample view, Stacey waited for the saga to unfold. She reached into her back pocket, pulled out her phone, and using the speed dial feature, called one of Austin's friends, Mike, who lived just a few houses down the street.

"Mike? It's Stacey, get out here. Austin's about to get into a fight with some guys from across town!"

Stacey hung up the phone and seconds later saw Mike bounding out his front door; wearing only his tattered blue jeans and plaid boxer shorts that were riding out from the top of his pants. Making eye contact with one another, Stacey simply pointed down the street towards the churches. Mike caught sight of the car sitting motionless in the middle of the road then made out Austin's silhouette cautiously walking down the sidewalk under the cover of darkness.

Stacey frantically tried dialing Austin's cell phone. When she heard the Ice T ringtone blaring inside the house, she knew that her effort was pointless and that all she could do now was watch and wait.

Peering around the evergreen, Stacey could see that Austin was now standing on the sidewalk, yelling obscenities at the driver. With an intent focus on the car, Stacey heard the engine rev, demonstrating its attitude as the car repeatedly lurched forward. The voices quieted to a rumble, making it difficult to hear who was saying what. With the whining of the engine, Stacey knew the situation was not becoming any less tense.

Stacey clasped her hands together and chewed on her thumbnails, a nervous habit she developed years ago, afraid to lose sight of Austin. As she waited for the resolution to finally come, Stacey's heart rate heightened as she watched Austin step off the sidewalk and slowly walk towards the driver's side of the angry piece of machinery. *What the hell is he doing?*

From the distance, Stacey watched intently as Austin walked up to the side of the car and leaned in to talk to the driver. *Maybe they're working it out.* she thought, the two appearing to now be engaged in a more civil conversation. Stacey dropped her hand and felt the tension in her chest ease as Austin now stood upright, his posture relaxed. *This will soon be over,* she convinced herself as Austin casually took a step back from the car and glanced back up the street at her.

The sudden thrust of orange flame out the side of the car took her by complete surprise. The flames, extending nearly to the sidewalk, mesmerized Stacey as she gasped at the horror as a vaporizing pink mist filled the air where Austin was standing. As the flames evaporated into the night, it left a trail of smoke that made it nearly impossible to see. The squealing of wheels riveted off of the brick walls of the churches as the car backed down the side street, out onto the main drag, and sped off to a new and unknown destination. Trying to put her body into motion, Stacey fought against her panic, frozen in time with complete and utter disbelief.

"AUSTIN! AUSTIN!!!" she cried out getting her feet in motion as she ran down the stairs and up the middle of the street. The momentum of time propelled slowly as Stacey forced one foot to follow the other, sprinting in slow motion to where she could now see Austin, lying in the middle of the street, blood flowing from his body, following the contour of the roadway into a nearby storm drain.

Looking down at her beloved, she could see the gaping hole in the side of his chest, the bloodied asphalt displaying through the wide cavity.

Austin's eyes twitched with the shock and pain as he

attempted to utter a few words. Kneeling down beside him, Stacey wrapped her arm behind his neck and bent her ear towards his mouth.

"What did you say?" she asked through her tears.

Once again, Austin tried to speak, but was only able to manage a gurgling noise through the blood now filling the back of his throat. Leaning his head off to the side, Austin stirred a gagging cough, freeing much of the blood from his throat.

Stacey leaned in closer and asked again, "What did you say?"

In a faint whisper, Austin reached deep within to muster as much strength as he could. With his last breath he looked up to see the tears streaming from Stacey's angelic face.

"I... I... love... you..."

****

Quiet settled over the car now reeking of gunpowder, blood, and mung, as it circled the beltway back to more familiar territory and pulled into a 24-hour car wash. Calvin pointed.

"There! Pull in there!"

Dave maneuvered the car into the complex as both of them looked around to ensure that neither people nor electronic surveillance equipment were present at the facility. Pulling the car into the bay furthermost from the roadway, Calvin got out from the passenger's seat. Grabbing the exterior of the doorpost and slamming the door shut, he felt a cool slimy sensation he immediately recognized as blood and muscle. He instinctively shook his hand in a frantic gesture to rid himself of the gory reminder of the life he had so effortlessly taken.

"That no good son of a bitch!" he yelled slamming his hand onto the hood of the trunk.

"What are we going to do?" Dave asked, stepping out from the driver's seat in complete dismay.

"We're going to wash off this car, and then find a place to hide! What the hell did *you* think we're gonna do? Go out and

44

find some other women? I ain't getting' no pussy tonight!" Calvin shouted sarcastically.

****

In due course, several neighbors called the 911 center, notifying the authorities of the shots fired. Marked units, stirred from their quiet midnight tour, sprinted to the scene, discovering Austin lying lifeless in his fiancée's arms in the middle of the road. In spite of the inevitable outcome, paramedics scooped Austin into the back of the ambulance and whisked him off to the St. Joseph Hospital, a world-renowned heart center, where doctors were able to clamp down the traumatized portions of the heart and revive a plausible heartbeat.

The heart surgeon meticulously sorted through the pieces, laying out the course of action.

"Looks like the blast missed the heart entirely, but we need to reconstruct the left pulmonary artery, it's completely gone—obliterated."

The surgical staff raced against the clock as they sutured the remnants of what remained back together and surgically inserted temporary makeshift vessels that could be replaced through a number of procedures at a later time. As the minutes continued ticking off the clock, the medical staff looked in complete amazement as Austin was able to maintain a steady sinus rhythm, the surgical table easily visible through his gaping chest wound.

"We've got to hurry people! We can't keep him clamped too much longer or he's going to v-fib!" the doctor announced as he continued knitting the infinitesimal pieces of the disorganized puzzle back together.

One nurse looked up at the clock, noting that Austin's life remained constant for the past twenty-two minutes. *How much longer can he hold on?*

A second surgeon made the necessary incisions into Austin's leg, retrieving viable veins to assist with the reconstruction. The pace heightened as the two sets of skilled hands miraculously recreated the system that would sustain life. As the threaded needle weaved through the torn vessels, one nurse, stationed off to the side monitoring the victim's vitals, raised the alarm.

"BP's falling fast! He's going to crash!"

"We're almost there!" the doctor said threading the needle through the last segment of torn tissue.

"Problem is, none of the vessels have firmed up their seal, he's leaking everywhere," the second surgeon noted.

Immediately the monitor's buzzer sounded, announcing that Austin's heartbeat had ceased. Knowing that CPR would be a futile attempt against the patchwork tirelessly reassembled, the doctor rested his hands on the side of the gurney and glanced up at the clock.

"We kept him alive for another forty-five minutes. It was a valiant attempt, but I'm calling this one. Nurse, please note the time of death at 2:21 a.m."

The doctor looked back down at the lifeless body, for the first time noticing just how young his patient truly was, dropping his head he meandered out from the operating room.

CHAPTER FIVE

Mingling through the late night traffic on the freeways to avoid drawing attention to themselves proved unbearable. Anxious to be through the miles that lay before them, the two friends sat quietly, glaring straight ahead as Calvin concentrated, both hands on the steering wheel. Sweat poured down their foreheads, the streams dripping down their faces and off the tips of their noses. Dave could not bear the silence any longer. Wiping the sweat from his brow he turned and asked, "So where are we going?"

"Hell if I know! I didn't exactly plan for the night to go this way!" Calvin said sharply.

As Dave looked at Calvin, his eyes drifted off through the driver's window and caught the set of headlights that slowly pulled alongside of them in the next lane. The darkly painted hood of the Lumina with the olive drab reflective stripe gave clear indication to the two not to draw any attention to themselves. The words "STATE POLICE" were clearly visible just outside the driver's window.

Calvin, seeing Dave's eyes swell like saucers, jerked his head to see what had caught his eye. He immediately made eye contact with the uniformed trooper, carefully inspecting their car. Dave was careful not to move erratically and felt confident they had cleaned the car rather well, leaving no evidence regarding the scene from which they were fleeing. However, as Dave looked down at the floorboard, he realized that neither he nor Calvin had thought of taking the time to better conceal the shotgun, or for that matter, to reload it from the earlier shooting.

"Damn! We weren't thinking," Dave said in a whisper to Calvin.

"What?" asked Calvin, now smiling at the trooper.

"If he pulls us over, we left the shotgun out and it isn't loaded! We wouldn't stand a chance!" Dave said.

"You mean shoot the trooper?" Calvin asked.

"Either we shoot him and get away—or go to jail!" Dave said.

"Kill a cop? You want me to kill a cop?" Calvin said almost losing his composure.

"What the hell? You blew that kid away back there! What do you have to lose?"

Calvin actually shuddered at how easy it was to pull the trigger in his moment of rage. Nevertheless, to kill a teenager and then get pulled over by one of Maryland's finest, then gun down a lawman would surely insure him a seat on death row. Calvin looked back at the trooper, gave a small grin and a nod of his head.

The trooper gave the car one last glance, punched his accelerator, and moved up the highway, outrunning the two unbeknownst felons.

"That was close!" Calvin said with great relief.

"All right, I know a place that we can go and hide for the night. Jump onto the Interstate and I'll show you how to get there," Dave said.

****

The marked cruisers cordoned off the block as red and blue lights refracted off of the two stone-faced churches. A crowd of neighbors gathered to find out more about the atrocity that had just transpired. Rumors filtered through the crowd rather quickly as some of the neighbors were privy to overhear the squabbling broadcasts given out over the police radios.

"I heard that they're looking for two guys armed with a shotgun," one neighbor told another.

"By the sounds of it" another neighbor interjected, "the victim didn't make it. They've got the homicide detectives on the way."

Not too long after the neighbor's prediction, Lang, Jones, and other members of the unit arrived on the scene, each wearing dark pinstriped suits, neckties and black trench coats. Each found his way behind the yellow crime scene tape stretched across the roadway a short distance behind the cruisers. It was always fascinating how the crowd became enthralled at the arrival of such distinguished officers, charged with investigating and identifying criminals responsible for one of the most reprehensible acts that could be committed on a fellow human being.

As Lang found his way to the middle of the street where Austin last stood, he could not help but wonder how prophetically peculiar the events were leading to Austin's death. Here was a young man, drawn to a section of the roadway between two churches, that professed the Gospel of Jesus Christ, and yet little was know as to whether or not Austin had ever spiritually prepared himself for eternity. *Most don't,* Lang thought as he looked upon the two steeples reaching high onto the night's sky. *Most simply think they will have all their life to live as they wish, then they'll 'get right with God' after they've grown old and gray and are lying on their death bed.* Lang shook his head at the mass of blood and mung strewn across the street. *I bet Austin never thought he'd die this young.* Lang thought quietly shifting his focus from the spiritual realm to the physical.

"Looks like we have two shotgun wads over here on the sidewalk," Jones announced, pointing towards his discovery. "And a shotgun blast into the hood of this Pontiac Grand AM," he concluded.

As the detectives gathered around the car to better inspect the damage each was astonished to find one single large gaping hole in the hood of the Pontiac.

"Looks like they shot him with a slug," Lang said with some dismay.

"They must have wanted him dead," said a curious uniformed officer.

"No doubt," Jones replied.

"Jonesy, did you see the handful of 25mm casings found over on the other side of the road?" Lang asked.

"No," he said suddenly peering toward that direction.

"Patrol placed a cone over them to protect them. Right over there." Lang said pointing with the end of his pen.

"Any word from the OR that the victim has more than one hole in him?" Jones asked.

"No, sir," answered another uniformed officer. "When we got on the scene he had one gaping hole through his chest. That's all the medics really said."

"All right, we'll we have crime lab here to document the scene. We need to get a search warrant for Austin's house later. Right now we need someone to secure his house while we take Stacey back to the office and interview her."

"10-4 man, you've got it!" answered the patrol officer who quickly coordinated other officers.

****

Huddled over a steaming cup of black coffee, Stacey adjusted the blanket that draped her shoulders as she sat quietly, staring out of the detective's office window watching the sunrise on her first day without her life mate. Stacey raised the cup to her nostrils and breathed in the aroma of the medium roast before taking a sip.

"Stacey, do you need something to eat?" Lang asked as he and Jones entered the office and tossed their trench coats across two different unoccupied chairs.

"Okay. I've had some time to cry, but don't think the reality has really struck me yet," she said offering a simple smile and taking another sip from the cup.

"Stacey, we talked back at the scene, but we'd like to get some of the details from you. The problem we have is that we can't prove that Calvin was involved in the murder. We know you met him at the reunion and that he started calling you on the cell phone, but there are no witnesses to say he was one of the two guys in the car that the shot came out of. We need to be able to prove beyond the shadow of doubt that Calvin was involved in the murder," Lang explained. "We could probably begin first by reviewing your cell phone and getting Calvin's cell phone number off of it along with the call history. That'll give us how many times he called you and hopefully, after we've subpoenaed his detail records, show him moving into the area," Lang explained.

Stacey set her steaming coffee off to the side and then set her purse square in the center of her lap. Parting the main zipper, she reached into the purse and extracted the Nokia cellphone. Pressing a button to illuminate the screen, Stacey commented how she noticed eleven new voicemail messages displaying on her screen. She quickly navigated to her caller history and noted that many of the calls were from friends who had undoubtedly heard the heart wrenching news of Austin's murder and were curious about her whereabouts and well-being. Using speed dial, Stacey quickly accessed her voicemails before surrendering her phone to Detective Lang for examination.

"Here," she said thrusting the phone out for Lang to take. "I can't stand listening to these messages."

Lang took the phone and carefully searched through the call history to retrieve the desired phone number. As he thumbed his way through the data, Jones reassured Stacey that they would certainly do everything in their power to identify, arrest and convict the persons responsible for Austin's murder.

"Whatever you need to help catch those bastards, you let me know!" she bolstered.

Having generated a list of the cell phone's call history, Lang compared the information to the times of the remaining voicemail messages that needed to be retrieved. One time stood out on its own. A phone call logged in at 1:15 a.m. had a matching voicemail that had yet to be opened. The phone number that it came from was the same number determined to belong to Calvin. Lang hit the voicemail speed dial and retrieved the messages. All, in fact, were friends who learned about Austin's demise sometime after 4:00 a.m. and wanted to express their grief, shock and sympathy. However, when Lang reached the voicemail of interest it came as no surprise to hear an agitated male caller screaming his vile threats onto the recorder. The caller seethed with envy and anger as he hurled his insults and threats to the "asshole" who found such great pleasure in mocking him.

Lang saved the message and quickly retrieved the body wire recording equipment, allowing him to preserve a copy of the message into digital format for repeated playback without any fear of the message becoming corrupted or degraded.

Securing the recording through a direct line, Lang looked up at Jones and said "Jonsey – you should hear this." Lang pressed the play button on the digital recorder and turned up the external speakers.

"Listen here you asshole! I'm on my way—"

"That's Calvin!" Stacey said briefly interrupting the message.

"I've got your route 72, 487, and Main Avenue bitch! Now get your ass outside! I got something for you, you no-good mother—" a loud metallic click resonated over the abrupt ending of the phone call.

"Did you hear that?" Lang asked.

"What?" Jones asked.

"That click—did you hear that?" Lang asked.

"Yeah, he hung up the phone on him." Jones said.

"No kidding. But he's on a cell phone and when you hang up on someone, you push a button. There's shouldn't be a loud click like your slamming the receiver down," Lang said.

"Okay, so what do you think it is?" Jones asked, half perturbed at the conversation.

"Sounds like the breach of a double-barrel shotgun slamming shut to me," Lang said.

Jones paused, considering the idea.

"Play it again."

Lang dialed in the position just a few seconds before the

clicking sound and pressed the play button.

Click.

The investigators played the sound several more times, leaning over the digital recorder and carefully listening to the amplified characteristics of the sound again. *Click.*

"Holy shit, Ken," Jones conceded, "you could be right. Tell you what; if we find a double-barrel shotgun I'll buy you a beer."

****

Earlier in the night, the car traversed through back roads and slowly crept by the gravel lane for the old one-story rancher. The twenty-year-old house sat quietly atop a wooded hill, a place allowing its occupants a panoramic view of the farmland countryside. There were no lights ignited around the property, which was not surprising at 4:25 in the morning. Nevertheless, if they didn't hurry, one of the neighboring farmers, heading out to the barn to milk their cows, may take notice of the unusual activity around the house and make an unnecessary phone call.

"What's it look like?" Dave sat intently inspecting for any possible signs that one of his family members may be staying the night.

"I don't know. I'll have to get a closer look to be sure the police aren't waiting to ambush us inside. I'll be right back."

Dave cautiously opened the car door and easily pushed it shut as Calvin lifted his hand and covered the interior light. Dave carefully walked up the tree line along the property's barbed wire fence that once allowed grazing cattle to feed off every corner of the property. Dave disappeared into the obscure gray shadows of the tangled woods.

Ducking in behind every large tree in order to conceal himself, Dave scurried up the narrow wood line until he reached the house. Circling the property, he quickly assessed that no one had stayed the night there, and more importantly, that the cops hadn't learned about the property. It would be a safe place for them to stay at least a day before moving on to another safe house.

"What took you so long?" Calvin demanded, concerned about the two cars that had already driven by his location.

"I had to make sure no one was there," Dave said climbing back into the passenger's seat. "Keep your lights off and head up the driveway. We'll hide the car in the garage around back."

Calvin quickly threw the transmission into second gear and spun around on the roadway to avoid using his reverse or braking lights. As they slowly wound up the quarter mile long driveway, they both noticed the kitchen light come on in the farmhouse next door. Pulling his foot off the accelerator and being careful not to touch the brakes, Calvin and Dave measured the probability of their discovery.

"I don't see anyone in the windows," Dave announced, motioning for Calvin to continue up the driveway.

The sedan pulled up and around the house to the empty three-car detached garage.

"Pull up to that door," Dave said, pointing to the first and closest door towards the house.

With great haste, Dave opened the garage door and let the car drift into the bay so they could begin emptying the contents. Like two prowlers making their way towards a new target, the two managed to walk through the dark lingering shadows, finding their way into the empty cottage retreat.

"So your dad owns this place, too?" Calvin asked.

"This is going to be our main home. He bought it about six months ago and has been renovating it through his construction company. When they have down time he sends workers up here to work on the house and pays them so they get a full day's pay," Dave explained.

"Shit, Dave! What if he has workers coming up in the morning or later in the day?" Calvin asked becoming irate.

"I'm always here when they're working—they won't know the difference," Dave answered.

Relieved with the answer Calvin found his way back to Dave's bedroom in the partially furnished million-dollar residence. As Calvin tossed his backpack at the foot of the bed, Dave carefully took the shotgun and placed it in the corner of his empty walk-in closet. Feeling somewhat secure, the two sprawled out in two different corners of the house, giving way to fatigue that had overwhelmed them the past few hours.

****

"Stacey, you said earlier at the house that from where you were standing on the front porch, it looked like there were two silhouettes in the car," Lang said recalling the earlier interview.

"Yeah!" she replied, affirming her account.

"So, if Calvin shot Austin, who's the other guy?" Lang asked.

Thinking back through the events from earlier that evening, Stacey sat quietly trying to recollect any associations of Calvin's from the past night, year or even during high school.

Stacey shook her head as she struggled with her memory. "No one comes to mind..."

"Stacey, who else was at Bateman's last night?" Jones asked.

Lost in thought, Stacey searched the faces from her recollection of the happier events that unfolded at the bar earlier that night. What she would give to rewind time and change the outcome knowing what she now knew. It was almost too much, trying to recall information while fighting back from mourning the loss of Austin. It seemed almost inhumane to ask one to put life on hold to provide information so that the victim's killer could be identified, tried and brought to certain justice. But none of that would come unless all possible vital information was divulged and processed. Stacey realized the importance of the detective's questions and with a renewed stamina grabbed her coffee and decided that she would remain in the homicide office until every nook and cranny of relevant information was explored.

"You know." Stacey said from a long quiet moment of deep intrinsic thought, "Calvin used to hang out with this Asian kid in high school named Dave... Dave Winslow."

Jones glanced up over his desk lamp as the new information came forth. He pulled his notebook to the center of his desk and flipped it open to a clean sheet of paper. Extracting a pen from his shirt pocket, Jones gave it a firm twist, and made notes on the information about the old high school friendship.

"They were almost never apart from one another. Calvin would always be at different places with Dave in tow," she said, allowing herself to laugh at the simple memory. "You know, we all graduated out of the same class and I haven't seen Dave since graduation day, but now that I think about it, I think someone mentioned something about Dave being there at Bateman's last night."

"Do you know where Dave lives?" Jones asked.

"No, but I know that his dad is Michael Winslow—you know—Winslow Homes? He's the owner," she added.

"The Winslow Homes that built all the new townhomes after all of the implosions downtown?" Jones asked.

"That's him. He lives somewhere out in the county somewhere near the reservoir. I've never been there," she said.

"What about a cell phone number for him? Would either you or your friends have that?" Jones asked.

Stacey considered for a moment where she would be able to secure Dave's cellphone number without compromising the case.

"Tricia would have it." she said. Quickly dialing her cell phone, Stacey contacted Tricia who graciously supplied the number and understood that secrecy was paramount to the success of the mission that now lay before the detectives.

Armed with both Calvin's and Dave's cell phone numbers, Jones prepared the required paperwork for completing the exigency request through their cellular carrier and faxed the official request for information that would divulge if Calvin and Dave's cell phones were in the same geographical area through the documented call history. Should the tower information prove what the detectives hoped it would, in conjunction with Stacey identifying the voice on the voicemail as belonging to Calvin, proving that these two were responsible for the murder of Austin would be less difficult than locating and apprehending them. With the advantage of a six-hour head start, the detectives realized that Calvin and Dave could be anywhere.

CHAPTER SIX

The two detectives arrived at the beautiful brick estate of Michael Winslow and his wife Linda; it was a magnificent display of architectural skill and craftsmanship. It had the appearance of something out of the 1700's with the cobble stone walkways, and the greening English ivy stretching up the entire face of the aged old home gave the impression of tradition, honor, and dignity. Mr. Winslow had been expecting their visit in spite of the earlier phone call confirmed he had not seen his son, Dave, for almost twenty-four hours. The wooden front door creaked open as the two detectives were escorted to the dinning room table where the three could sit comfortably and discuss the matter over piping hot tea that awaited their arrival.

"Mr. Winslow, I'm sure this may be rather difficult for you, but I appreciate you taking time out of your day to speak with us," Jones said opening the dialog.

"What exactly is this about?" Mr. Winslow demanded. "You wouldn't tell me over the phone."

"Mr. Winslow, last night there was a murder near the Towson area, a young man, Austin Michaels, was shot and killed by a Calvin Hampton. We're investigating that murder. We've learned that Calvin and your son Dave are close friends and have reason to believe that Calvin may now be putting

Dave into harm's way," Jones said, somewhat deceivingly.

"Dave? Are you saying that my Dave participated in this murder?" Mr. Winslow asked rather alarmed.

"Sir, please hear me. I am saying that Dave may have been there when the shooting occurred, but right now, I am more concerned about the well-being of your son. Do you know where he is?" Jones asked very pointedly.

"Well, I have another house we purchased out near the county line that I'm currently renovating. Because it's nearly finished we sometimes stay there different days throughout the week. But we haven't been there in the last few weeks," he explained.

"Mr. Winslow, I'm compelled to ask you this next question – do you have any guns in the house?" Lang asked.

Mr. Winslow acknowledged first with a headshake, followed by a more definite reply, "Yes. Yes I do! But they should all be here."

"Mr. Winslow, would you be so kind as to check your inventory and confirm that all you guns are accounted for, please?" Lang asked.

"Absolutely." he replied as he excused himself from the table and worked his way upstairs.

The two detectives sat quietly as they heard Mr. Winslow console his wife who was sitting upstairs, weeping as she heard her son's plight unfold from the detectives seated at her dining room table. Not knowing what news the detectives intended bringing, she had not joined the meeting as she couldn't bear the agony of hearing any dreadful news.

He was a model student despite the difficult adjustments after his overseas adoption some ten years earlier. Mr. and Mrs. Winslow, who were active in their local church, felt God had blessed them financially so that they could help provide good homes to unfortunate orphans from the remnants of the ancient Roman territory. After adopting two Russian girls and having a girl of their own, the Winslow's wanted a son and sought to fulfill that desire by starting the adoption process again. Several years later and after spending a small fortune traveling back and forth from Romania, Dave came to be the

Winslow's fourth child.

Mr. Winslow returned to the dining area. As he rounded a corner and made his way back to the waiting detectives, Jones and Lang both noticed the drawn, concerned look washing over his face. Standing behind the dining room chair where he braced his stance, Mr. Winslow could barely make the statement.

"After looking through my armory, it appears that I am missing one gun... a double barrel shotgun. It's an older, breech loading model."

I thought so.

****

Lieutenant Holmes entered the briefing room wearing his dark blue jumpsuit, duty belt with his SigSauer handgun mounted on his hip, carrying the standard Motorola police radio, appropriately tuned into the side secret channel. As commander of the Tactical Unit, Lt. Holmes never felt the need to acquire any specialized training with the elite tactical weapons. He always felt safe and comfortable around those men who were not only proficient with such weaponry, but who had also achieved a lifetime of military training experience through a variety of Special Forces. Lt. Holmes' objective was to simply deploy his tactical column, render the house safe, and apprehend the suspects without incident. For this reason, he insisted on being involved in the development of every operations plan.

"We'll need both squads for this one sir." Sergeant Cowley said after already being briefed on the essential information.

"Why's that?" Lieutenant Holmes asked.

"We have two possible homicide suspects penned up in a sprawling rancher that sets a quarter mile off the road, on a twenty acre wooded lot, with lots of opportunities to ambush us. I'd like to deploy at least two snipers after night fall and let them gather intel for at least two hours before insertion. The property is so big that we need to break down into three teams: one for the perimeter and two for the breaching. If we can hit the front and the back corner entrances simultaneously, we should be able to get in safely, overwhelm them, and have them neutralized before they can make a counteroffensive."

"Flash-bangs?" asked the Lieutenant.

"Absolutely," replied the sergeant.

"Very good. I would only suggest we have our armored vehicle on standby should things go south."

"Consider it done, lieutenant," Sergeant Cowley replied.

With the sun already falling behind the edge of the horizon, time was of the essence for the officers who would be breaching the house to apprehend the two wanted murder suspects. The long, dark, panel van was loaded with the snipers and to their relief, officers who donned their Ghillie suits, then unloaded and assembled their McMillan A3 sniper rifles and scopes. With their equipment in place and all systems go, the van drove past the long, winding driveway of the target address, slowing enough for the panel door to slide open as two snipers and their assistants slipped out the side, quickly hiding discreetly in a wooded area. With only a quarter mile to cover, the two teams covered the distance quickly and quietly, reporting via the radio's secured channel over which they had established their positions within 10 minutes of deploying. As each surveyed his area of responsibility, none observed any signs of the house currently being occupied.

Observing the residence for at least an hour, both snipers, after thoroughly inspecting every visible inch of the residence through their high-powered scopes, determined the house was most likely empty, and that the present time afforded them the best opportunity to secure the residence. Lt. Holmes concurred. With that confirmation, the three squads of men lined up and moved out towards their objective. Just as their predecessors did, the three squads jumped from the side of the van and worked through the narrow tree line. Two of the teams ascended the hill to the house. Team-three deployed around the perimeter, setting their sites on the windows and doors most likely to be used in an escape. Teams one and two found their breaching point, hunkered down, and waited for the radioed command to begin their ballet of violence.

"All teams are in place and are awaiting your order, Sir," the Sergeant radioed to Lt. Holmes.

As the radio squelched to silence, Lieutenant Holmes said a quick prayer for each of his men. Knowing that he was placing them into harm's way, this simple ritual gave him great comfort. With his final 'Amen,' he pulled the radio to his mouth and squeezed the push-to-talk button.

"Execute. I say again—execute," came the order.

Like clockwork, the two breaching officers rammed their respective doors, splintering them open, as the third officer in each stick pulled the pins from their grenades and tossed the exploding devices through the entryways.

"...8, 9, 10!" counted an officer as the entire team shielded their eyes and waited for the explosion.

The tactical officer reached ten exactly when the two explosions resounded with a boom that flexed every window in the house, echoing across the cornfields, signaling to entry teams it was time to make haste. Team one filtered in through the front door and covered the living room, dining room and kitchen areas as team two made their entry through a side entrance that gave easy access to the nearby bedrooms and baths. Having the opportunity to see a hand-drawn floor plan of the residence during their briefing, each officer was very familiar with his area of responsibility. They flowed throughout the rooms of the house scanning every corner with their MP5 submachine guns and M16 rifles.

"Living room, clear," cried out one officer. "Clear in the master bedroom," yelled another. Similarly the 'all clear' calls came from different areas of the house, giving satisfaction that the residence was thoroughly searched and determined safe.

Having cleared the main floor, a secondary team formed up behind the bunker that stood at the top of the basement steps. With a stick of eight men, the basement door flung open and the bunker shimmied down the stairway into the cold dank area.

"All clear," came the final cry.

****

62

In only a matter of moments after the all clear sounded, the tactical unit had every light in the house illuminated as a multitude of detectives; command staff, support staff, and Mr. Winslow worked their way up the driveway to further this investigation.

Sergeant Cowley found Detective Jones and told him about an important discovery that his team uncovered while clearing one of the bedroom closets. Wanting to see the discovery for himself, Detective Jones walked into the residence and found the specific room the good sergeant described. Leaning in the corner of the vacant closet was a double-barrel breech-loading shotgun, freshly cleaned.

Mr. Winslow rounded the corner to find Detective Jones staring at the find. Catching his eye, Jones turned and asked the homeowner "Would that be your missing shotgun?"

"Why, yes! Yes it is!"

****

Through their search of the residence pursuant to the authorized search warrant, investigators logically worked their way through the residence, searching for any clues that would harden the case against Calvin and Dave, as well as looking for any indications as to where they may have fled. As detectives concentrated on Dave's bedroom where the shotgun of interest was located, careful attention surrounded a small duffel bag lying haphazardly on the floor. Peering into the side pocket with his flashlight, Jones pushed the flap open a little further where a glint of light flared back at him, captivating his interest. Clamping the mini-mag flashlight between his lips, Jones parted the opening further with his gloved hands, finding a handful of loose 25mm ballpoint rounds at the bottom of the pocket, intermingled with a few unfired 2 ¾" shotgun slugs. Upon closer examination, Jones noted t the slug cartridges were of the same make and style as those found at the shooting scene.

The remainder of the house left little, if any, clues about

the two felons who were on the run. Discarded soiled plates confirmed they finally regained their appetite while the empty garage further conveyed to detectives the two may be driving around in Dave's 2002 Mazda Protégé. But then again, it would seem prudent to lose that car if it were the car used at the time of the murder.

A 'be on the look out' (BOLO) continued being aired over the police frequencies from the night before, giving no new or updated information. The detectives worked frantically, placing the 2002 Mazda Protégé in the NCIC national database as a "felony vehicle" and chased down computer record checks of family and associates for the two wanted fugitives. Lang ran the assorted variables that presented themselves as endless streams of information that continued to flourish regarding Calvin's criminal record. The minor brushes with the law already brought forth a number of names and aliases he had used during prior arrests. Cross-checking the information through other databases proved quite tedious and time consuming;, however, as Lang narrowed down the possibilities, one immediate piece of information stood out above all the rest.

"Hey, Jonesy. Did you know Calvin actually used his brother's name on a traffic stop two years ago when he got locked up for DWI?" Lang said.

"No! Where does his brother live?" asked the inquisitive detective.

"Funny you should ask. His brother Charles lives just over the county line, not too far from the house we just raided. I wonder if he's staying there?" Lang posed.

"There's only one way to find out."

Surveilling this residence would prove to be difficult for the specialized surveillance team, whose sole task was to locate and apprehend such serious offenders. Like the first hideout, this one was also a ranch-style house located on a dead-end road behind a grove of pine trees that gave detectives little to observe from up the road. What made the task most difficult was the remoteness of the residence. Unfamiliar cars in the neighborhood sitting along the side of the country roads would cause concerned citizens to telephone the local sheriff's department. Having an influx of marked police units in that region of the neighboring county would chase the fugitives off to a new and unknown location.

"What about going up on their phones?" the detective asked of his sergeant.

"We already checked their phones – they've dumped them. We'll have to find them the old-fashioned way" answered the sergeant.

"If we can place him in the house recently, the homicide boys might be able to get a search warrant for this location," offered the detective.

"They're working on that now. They've found a friend of the boys who is going to place a covert call to Charles' house, posing as if he is looking to talk with Calvin. If whoever answers the phone tells him to call back at a certain time, well, then we'll hit the place with the Maryland State Police SWAT team when they're home," the sergeant explained.

The covert call was placed, but it failed to yield the information the detectives hoped. The friend was able to learn that Calvin and Dave stayed there the night before, but according to Charles, wasn't sure if they would be staying again that night as the two had ventured out to find some long desired ale and women.

Nonetheless, investigators finally developed enough information to concentrate the surveillance efforts around the vicinity of the newly acquired residence. By concealing undercover cars around the local firehouse, garage, and general store, the surveillance team established a perimeter around their new target location. Dividing the twenty-four hours of required coverage between the two squads, each team would man their post for twelve long hours before seeing any relief. Undercover detectives would relieve the prior shift, take up their position, and sit and wait for any profitable activity. The futile exercise continued for forty-eight hours, but unfortunately, no new intel came in and Lang and Jones were now left with a crucial decision.

"With the covert phone calls we can say the suspects were in that house in the last forty-eight hours and that it's possible evidence could be in there," Lang explained. "I think we would be remiss if we didn't try to secure a search warrant to seize any potentially valuable evidence."

"I agree," Jones replied. "We're still looking for a 25mm handgun and there has got to be some bloody clothing somewhere."

****

This time the pre-ops meeting took place on the hood of an unmarked Chevy Lumina that bore the familiar police radio antennas and concealed dash lights. Members of the Maryland State Police SWAT Team, armed with the staple bunker, ram, halogen tools, rifles, and submachine guns, circled the front of the Lumina to gain a quick birds-eye glance of the plan that was being sketched out on the legal pad.

"We do things just a bit differently out here," the MSP SWAT sergeant announced to Lang. "We need you to join us on the stick. Your job is to follow the team up to the property and point out the actual house that you've named in the search warrant. Then, hold the perimeter while we make entry."

"You want me to hold the perimeter by myself?" Lang asked considering the various avenues of escape for the two-acre piece of property.

"You'll have some help from above," the sergeant said. "Okay, boys, let's move out."

In the back of a dark panel van similar to the one the tactical unit had used when deploying their team, Lang was shown his seat at the end of a wooden bench that ran the course of the van's length, much like a jump seat in an old World War II 'war bird' designed to outfit paratroopers. Each of the troopers filed in, took up their position, and slammed the door shut. As the van inched its way under the cover of darkness, each member of the assault team conducted the necessary radio checks through the communication devices secured within their Kevlar helmets.

"Have you ever done an entry?" one of the troopers asked of Lang.

"Many times. In fact, except in homicide, we do all of our own entries unless there is something overtly dangerous in someone's background; then we call out our Tactical Unit," Lang replied.

"Good. So you know what to do if the shit hits the fan?" he said.

"Don't worry about it – I've got your back," Lang said with a wink.

The van crept to a slow stop, behind a tree line, within feet of the driveway's entrance. The panel door slid open cautiously, so as not to cause any sudden unfamiliar noises, and the members of the SWAT team dropped out of the van with Lang bringing up the rear. As the team scurried along the line of trees that stretched down the drive, the new moon glistened from above, casting the team's long shadows over the center of the roadway.

"This is it. This is our target," Lang said, pointing directly at the rancher.

Reaching the corner of the property, the team leader positioned Lang in the shadows of a tall aged pine. Clad in a dark suit and a long black overcoat, Lang immediately became obscure in the shadows as he took careful aim with his .40 caliber SigSauer, covering potential threats from the bedroom windows for the now advancing team.

In the few seconds it took the team to cover the edges of the front yard, a high pitched noise crescendoed from somewhere behind Lang's position. It swelled in swiftly, startling the detective.

Trooper 1, the Maryland State Police Dauphine helicopter swooped in and hovered only feet from the target's rooftop. The magnificent bird hovered overhead, its search light abruptly ignited and blazed, pouring over the entire property; its blinding light jerking back and forth, checking each of the entrances and exits.

"This is the Maryland State Police! We have the house surrounded! Come out with your hands up or we will come in. I say again, come out with your hands up or we're coming in," the overhead PA system blared above the intensity of the rotor wash that gusted down against the house causing the roof shingles to appear like gentle waves at sea.

"No response, Sarge!" one teammate stated.

"Go! Go! Go!" the order came as the Sergeant waived the signal to 'execute' with his left hand.

As one trooper applied the halogen tool to the locked screen door and effortlessly tore it away from its frame, another applied one swift swing of the ram that plundered the wooden door, splintering it as the team converged into the darkened abode. In that very instant a tremendous explosion with a brilliant white flash radiated from the depth of the house which prompted the repeated screaming of "Police, search warrant." The dancing light beams on the drawn shades of the windows in each room allowed Lang to trace the progress of the team as they breached and cleared their target. In a manner of minutes, the 'all clear' was confirmed; interior lights were turned on, and the Dauphine helicopter lifted off to a higher elevation, returning to its hanger where it would return to service, awaiting its next medevac assignment.

Lang holstered his service weapon and made his way through the cool night air to the front door where he was greeted by the team members exiting the residence.

"Sorry – it's empty" said one trooper, his MP5 freely swinging about from its strap.

Aggravated, Lang pulled his cell phone out from his coat pocket, flipped open the communications device, and chirped up Jones who stood anxiously waiting for word.

"What do we have?" Jones asked, answering the chirp.

"Nothing! The house is empty. Looks like we need to make these guys stars on the local news. Let's get a hold of the Public Information Office and let everyone know that they're wanted for murder."

"10-4."

CHAPTER SEVEN

Gwendolyn placed the key into her deadbolt and turned it clockwise, allowing her third story apartment door to swing open. Stepping in, she pushed the door closed as she lumbered to the kitchen, her arms straining to get the three bags of groceries onto the counter. Walking back through the living room she noticed the red blinking light on her answering machine. Stepping over to the scarred pressboard end table, Gwendolyn reached down and clicked the play button.

"Hey, Gwen! It's me. I know you said that you didn't want me calling you anymore, but I'd really like it if you gave me a fair chance. I think we'd be good together. You've got my number on the caller ID; give me a call sometime—please?" When the message ended, Gwendolyn glared at the recording device, offered her best-calloused smirk, and promptly hit the delete button. *This guy just won't quit!*

****

Detective Keith Winthrop sat quietly at his desk, muddling through the required paperwork from his latest SIDS death investigation; genuinely on the up and up. Affixing his signature to the final supplementary report, Winthrop tossed his pen before fishing out a Marlboro cigarette from the box stashed in his jacket pocket.

"I'm heading out for a smoke break. Let me know if anything happens," he said, the cigarette bobbing up and down in his mouth while he spoke.

Each of the other detectives continued about their work catching up loose ends on biology requests, autopsy reports, and quick telephone updates with family members still seeking a resolution in their loved-ones case.

Winthrop returned to the office, the cigarette smell lingering behind him as he walked through the squad room. Adjusting the volume knob on his police radio, the Seventh Precinct erupted with chattering commotions that left the road officers quite frazzled.

"What's happening on channel seven?" Lang asked.

"Sounds like a working apartment fire across town. They've got the avenue shut down near the junction. I wouldn't be going home that way if I were you," he offered with a large grin.

****

The four-alarm fire paralyzed the county's fire department assets, rendering most engines and trucks that typically safeguarded the central district out of service. The strain reached the outer most corners of the region as the condensed firehouses were suddenly responsible for covering a larger region, at least until the trucks were relieved of their duty and back in service. Since the first engine to arrive immediately radioed for additional alarms as the flames poured through the roof of the third story apartment and licking the cool dark night sky, firefighters abroad knew that tonight would be long and grueling.

The displaced tenants from the apartments gathered around the nearest corner, huddling into a circle, comforting one another as the firefighters pulled the hoses from the truck beds, stretched them out down the road and made the connections to hydrants. A group of firefighters, their faces obscured by the reflection of the flames dancing across their masks, walked past an eight-year-old boy who stepped away from his family's side to take in the startling scene. The teams of two each grabbed a line, checked to ensure that the pressure was free flowing with a quick squirt from the nozzle and ascended the three flights of stairs heaving the weighted hoses over their shoulders.

The young boy watched intently as the firefighters braced themselves on each side of the door. Another firefighter quickly made an entrance by prying the door open with his halogen tool, allowing the flames to suddenly make an escape, engulfing the third-floor landing. Turning their backs to shield themselves from the flashback, the two teams engaged their hoses and turned into the doorway. As their silhouettes disappeared into the flames, the youngster appreciated the bravery of the men committed to saving his house; in that instant he knew what he wanted to be when he grew up.

The fire raged for several hours before the firefighters brought it under control. The area captain approached the battalion chief with the update for the news crews emerging on the scene.

"We've got it contained. It should be out within the next forty-five minutes. However, it looks like we have a fatality. One occupant in the apartment was found dead in the bathtub," said the captain.

"Smoke inhalation?" asked the battalion chief.

"It's hard to tell. She's lying in her bathtub, nude. I've already contacted the comm center liaison to notify the county police and have the Arson and Homicide Units respond. We'll let them make that call."

"Very good, Captain. Let's finish putting out that fire and wrap it up!"

****

Fire fatalities were the rare occasion where two squads, the Homicide Unit and the Arson Unit, would work the investigation. Together, with each concentrating on their specialty, the Arson Unit would lend their expertise in determining the origin and path of the destructive blaze while the Homicide Unit looked for any foul play. Should the fire appear genuine, or accidental, then the Arson Unit would show the responsibility of the investigation. However, if the fire appeared to be an arson that led to the death of the resident, the Homicide Unit would carry the criminal investigation, relying on the arson specialists to lend their expertise.

With the infrequency of fatal fires, it was not too often that homicide detectives were required to respond. But, given the nature of such investigations to inevitably have a slow start, the unit would dispatch as many detectives as possible should the event turn out to be an actual homicide.

As the detectives from the two squads converged on the scene, the fire department finished rolling up the last water line, lugging it back to its cargo hold on the truck.

"What do you have, Charlie?" asked Winthrop as he lit a cigarette.

"One fire—one dead girl. According to the leasing office Gwendolyn Morgan is the sole tenant of apartment E. She's single, employed with Verizon Wireless, and has no children. Based on the description her neighbors gave us, it sounds like she'll be your dead girl in the bathtub," the fire Captain said.

"Has the family been notified yet?" Winthrop asked.

"Nope. We just put out the fires. All that other 'police-like stuff we leave for you." said the Captain with a nod of his head.

"All right, Charlie, if putting out fires is all you can handle, then we'll get on with figuring out the rest of it. Any idea where the fire started?" Winthrop asked.

"Looks like the bathroom though, I can't say I've ever seen a fire start in the middle of a floor. No ignition source, of course, unless one was put there," the Captain said as he pulled out his own pack of cigarettes and lit one up.

"Easy enough. How soon before we can go in and search?"

"The boys are almost done; they should be out any minute."

"Thanks, Captain."

****

There was something comical about seeing a soft-shoe detective climb into his fire department-issued turnout gear so as not to soil the JC Penney Stafford special. Yet they prepared to scale the three flights of stairs to enter the scorched ruins by slipping on their bib overalls, knee-deep boots, and reflective fire coats.

The color from each room had been erased as the heat and smoke damage filtered through every corner of the apartment, rendering it much like an antique photograph. Winthrop, Lang, and Jones sifted through the charred debris, searching for any clues that would immediately identify the nature and cause of the fire. Melted pictorial remnants intermingled across the dampened floor with the burnt framework of a once beautiful Victorian floral print sofa and chair, giving indication to the detectives that should this investigation turn criminal, good direct physical evidence would certainly be hard to come by.

Jones wandered into the unscathed bedroom and stood amazed at how the sweltering heat from the inferno buckled the oak headboard, dresser, and night stands. As morning's light streamed in through the bedroom windows, Jones started his search in the far corner with the nightstand. *Usually don't find much in these kinds of scenes.* Pulling the top drawer open he found only one item. A 'Thinking of You' Hallmark card featuring a print of an oil painting of a bouquet of flowers setting on a tabletop draped in fine linen. Feeling the delicacy of the card that barely withstood the elements of the fire, Jones opened the card and read the contents.

"THINKING OF THAT SPECIAL SOMEONE TODAY" filled the interior in a pastel blue ink. But written by hand was an addendum penned by the sender, "Hoping we can get to know each other better. Have a blessed day! Sincerely, pj356@iemail.com."

Strange, he didn't sign his name.

Meanwhile, Lang scoured through heaps of blistered debris, piled in two different corners of the living room. Pushing aside the remnants of a throw pillow, Lang's attention was drawn towards a blackened, leather bound book with only the right bottom corner singed, leaving most of the pages quite legible. Pulling the book from the pile of debris, Lang swiped his latex covered hand over the cover; "THE HOLY BIBLE" appeared softly through smoke damage. Seeing that the bookmark tassel was marking a particular reference, Lang turned to the page, his eyes falling on the underlined passage: "Yea, though I walk through the valley of the shadow of death, I will fear no evil: for thou art with me; thy rod and thy staff they comfort me. Thou preparest a table before me in the presence of mine enemies: thou anointest my head with oil, my cup runneth over." Reverently closing the book, Lang contemplated the passage from Psalm 23 and wondered what good could come from a life cut so short; what purpose did this death have in God's greater plan? Though Lang realized that answers to his questions may never come on this side of eternity, he paused a moment to imagine how twenty-two year old Gwendolyn Morgan was spending her first few hours in Heaven.

****

Pulling the overhead lamp in closer, Medical Examiner Dr. Jonathan Resnick squinted carefully to be certain about his examination.

"I am absolutely sure," he said with utmost confidence. "Even though the hands are badly burned, I can say with all medical certainty that her fingertips have been cut off. They're missing."

"Are you sure, Doc?" Winthrop asked.

"Positive." came the firm reply. "I've already examined much of the exterior of the body. There are no bullet holes or stab wounds. We'll get her cleaned the best we can to look for any blunt force trauma. Then, I'll dissect her throat. That should tell us a great deal about whether or not she was alive at the time the fire started. For now, we'll get her toxicology and vaginal swabs to see if she was sexually assaulted," Dr. Resnick explained.

"Okay, Doc. But just so you know, we're already fourteen hours into this and we still don't know if it's a homicide or accidental death. I need some direction," Winthrop responded.

"Give me five minutes to finish collecting the blood samples and swabs, and I'll get right on it."

****

With the intensity that often accompanied such investigations came the need for a short respite and a good hot breakfast. And the Penn Street Diner, located immediately across from the Medical Examiner's Office, always provided a home-cooked breakfast and a little time to roundtable the investigation.

"Anything else I can get you fellows?" the waitress asked as she finished setting the orders out for each of the investigators.

"I think we're good," Winthrop said with a huge smile followed by a wink.

"What are you thinking?" Lang asked.

"I think we got a murder and that we're getting further behind the eight-ball the longer we wait. Seems like this doctor isn't in any big hurry."

"We've already interviewed all the neighbors, nobody seemed to know her; she only lived there for about six months," Jones offered.

"I can jump on the court order for the email provider for 'pj356.' But I'm wondering, was her home phone voicemail set up on the actual phone, or is it off site through her landline provider?" Lang asked.

"I don't know, but if you can find out that would be great. And Jonesy, do me a favor, start writing a search warrant for the apartment," Winthrop said.

"What are you looking for?" Jones asked.

"Her fingertips. They've gotta be somewhere in that apartment."

"Are you thinking they may have tried to flush them?"

"Damn straight. Hopefully they got caught in the drain trap instead of heading out the main sewer line. Also, I want to try and swab the front door knob for any possible DNA. I'm hoping that whoever was in the apartment with Gwendolyn last touched the door knob and left something," Winthrop said.

"I don't know," Jones offered with some doubt. "This new stuff with 'touch DNA' can be more complicated than you think, especially when the touch DNA sample you're getting is from a public place, like the exterior part of a door knob where any 'Joe Shmoe' could have touched it. If it comes back positive for someone else's DNA, someone who had nothing to do with her death, it could come back to bite you in the ass in court." Jones explained.

"I know Jonesy, but it's all we have," answered Winthrop.

****

As it turned out, Winthrop's speculation about being too far behind the eight-ball was truer than he realized. Having returned to the autopsy room after concluding his respite at the Penn Street Diner, Winthrop would be present when Dr. Resnick made the initial incision for the dissection of the trachea and meticulously made his way deep, exposing the hyoid bone structure.

"I couldn't see this from all the burning on the outside, but this confirms it. Her hyoid bone is broken. Look! Even her thyroid and cricoid cartilage is all broken up. No doubt, she was strangulated at some point. We'll have to cut deeper to see if there is any smoke in her trachea."

The doctor continued carving deeper into the lifeless cadaver, laying open her throat, exposing the lower trachea region that would signify for certain whether her death was caused by the intense smoke or whether she died at the hand of another.

"Ah," he said holding each side wide open. "You see? There's no smoke in the trachea. So she didn't breath in any smoke while the fire was burning in the apartment. Therefore, I'm ruling the cause of death is asphyxiation by strangulation and the manner of death is homicide. Now detective, you can move on with your investigation and find her killer."

****

Having written the necessary paperwork, Lang and Jones walked up the granite stone stairway at the Circuit Court's building. Showing their credentials to the sheriff's deputies, bypassing the security screening process, they split into two different directions. Lang scooted over to the elevators and pressed the up button to summon the next car that would carry him to the State Attorney's Office who would authorize the subpoena demanding account and subscriber information that would hopefully reveal who "pj356@iemail.com" was and perhaps reveal further information that would identify Gwendolyn's killer.

Meanwhile, Jones darted left towards the stairwell and bounded up to the third floor where he found the day's chambers judge, Thomas Henderson Sr., practicing his golf putting as he aimed the next dimpled ball towards the simulated hole—an old Budweiser beer glass lying on its side.

"Come on in, Detective," the judge said as the ball clanked, striking the inside of the glass. "I'm getting ready for the BAR Association's golf tournament set for next month. With all the free beer and the bad golfing, I thought I'd take advantage of my fellow constituents' lust for the brew and get in a good golf score while they become inebriated. Then I'll join them at the days' end. So, what do you have for me today?"

"Your honor, I have an application and affidavit for a search and seizure warrant for a murder that occurred last night," Jones answered.

"Really? Where did the murder happen?" asked the judge setting his favorite putter up against the wooden bookshelves bearing his personal legal library.

"Here in the central district, down by the city line. There was a fatal fire at an apartment complex last night that has turned out to be a murder," Jones explained.

"I remember seeing the fire on the news and hearing about the fatality, what makes it a murder?" asked the judge.

"According to the ME, she was strangled and already dead before the fire started. We've also noted that her fingertips were cut off. Not sure why, but they left her in her own apartment, so identifying her was rather simple, with or without her fingertips," Jones said.

Judge Henderson's countenance fell as he took the affidavit and read about the unfortunate circumstances that befell Gwendolyn Morgan the previous night.

"Detective, please raise your right hand," Judge Henderson requested.

Jones immediately complied.

"Do you affirm, under the penalties of perjury, that the statements made in this application are the truth and the whole truth?"

"I do, your Honor."

And at the stroke of a pen, Judge Thomas Henderson Sr. authorized members of the police department to return to the fire scene, further processing it for any potentially missed evidence.

Exiting the stairwell into the main foyer of the courthouse, Jones spotted Lang standing off to the side waiting for his return.

"What took you so long?" Lang asked.

"The judge was playing putt-putt up in his chambers," Jones answered. "You get the subpoena?"

"Yep. And I faxed it off from the States Attorney's Office. We should have the information in the ten minutes it'll take us to drive back to the office."

"Well, let's get moving!"

****

The two detectives returned to the office with Lang circling around the fax machine to see if the promise at the corporate offices for the email provider had been kept. Lang pulled a stack of papers off the communal facsimile device that serviced one corner of the 10th floor at police headquarters. Some one-hundred detectives, ranking officers, and administrative staff shared the device, so pedaling through the paperwork took a few moments to sort and stick into the appropriately marked basket so that other information would reach its intended destination.

As expected Lang found his response to his subpoena as the last in the pile. Flipping past the traditional cover sheet, Lang scanned the account information for pj356@iemail.com as he walked through the rear office door and into the squad room.

"So, who's our mystery lover?" Winthrop asked from his corner desk.

"James Calvin Woodridge the third." Lang answered.

"Are you shitting me?" Winthrop demanded.

"Nope. His date of birth is 3/18/1956... and get this, he lives—"

"In apartment C! Right below Gwendolyn Morgan's apartment," Winthrop said finishing Lang's sentence for him. "But we know him as Assistant Bishop James C. Woodridge III of the Center for Glorious and Abundant Life Church. Jonesy talked to his wife last night."

"Yes I did. And you know what? That no good son of a bitch is married and has three kids," Jones said.

"So, I don't get it?" Winthrop said.

"Get what?" Lang asked.

"Where's he get 'pj356' from?"

"I bet he goes by 'Pastor Jim!'" Lang offered. "For some people, titles are everything. The head bishop at the church probably wants that title for himself and requires the assistants to use 'pastor' to distinguish the pecking order," Lang said.

"Well... pastor, bishop, whatever the hell he is, we need to get into his life and find out what the hell happened last night," Winthrop said, slamming his notebook down on his desktop.

"So where was the good bishop last night when the fire broke out?" Lang asked.

"He was treating the missus to a fine dinner while the kids were at the babysitter's house," Jones replied without having to confer with his notes.

"At 9:30 p.m.?" Lang asked.

"Hey, when you're a bishop, you can afford to eat with the rich," said Winthrop.

CHAPTER EIGHT

The pressure finally mounted with Calvin, Dave, and their families. With the police executing several search warrants at a variety of family homes, compounded by the recent local news coverage depicting these two young men as heinous killers, Mr. Winslow retained the services of one of the most prestigious criminal attorneys in the Baltimore metropolitan region. Matt Anderson, Esq., Attorney at Law, contacted the homicide office and inquired about arranging to have the two suspects surrender themselves into police custody.

"That sounds quite reasonable, Mr. Anderson, but as you are well aware, we have a search warrant for Randy's 2002 Mazda Protégé. If we find out that anyone has been intentionally concealing the whereabouts of this car, we intend to prosecute them for hindering the criminal investigation. And, I feel pretty certain Mr. Winslow wouldn't want any such backlash causing negative repercussions on his construction business. Such negative press could seriously impact his ability to be regarded as an upright businessman here in the Baltimore area," Jones explained.

"I see," Anderson said. "I'll make every effort to have the two turn themselves in by noon tomorrow. I'll see what I can do about locating this missing car."

****

With Bishop James Calvin Woodridge's flirtatious conduct raising everyone's eyebrows in the homicide office; it went without saying that extreme caution would have to be measured when executing the search warrant above his apartment. Though he, like the other families, was displaced by the water and smoke damage from the fire, surveillance teams conveyed to the homicide investigators that many of these displaced tenants were in and out of their apartments, getting necessities and valuables moved to their new locations. Since the apartment complex owned three different properties throughout the central portion of the county, the detectives were hoping to have Bishop Woodridge and his family as far away from the complex as possible. But such wouldn't be the case as the detectives and the crime lab unit moved in to begin salvaging every last piece of evidence possible.

Winthrop walked up to apartment C and knocked on the door.

"Mr. Woodridge, it's Detective Winthrop, could I have a moment of your time?" The bishop pulled the door open further and allowed Detective Winthrop to step inside. Just as the door closed, Winthrop intentionally took a step back and braced himself against the door, to prevent the bishop from learning that the investigators were moving into the upstairs apartment to swab the door knobs, pull the drainage pipes from beneath the toilet, and extract any fruitful evidence enumerated in the search warrant.

"Mr. Woodridge, are you guys staying here?" asked Winthrop.

"No, the leasing office moved us to an apartment around the corner, we're just here getting stuff we need. They took good care of us, the main office that is. They had our laundry professionally cleaned and were able to get us basic furniture in the new place. We just needed some dishes and baby stuff that we left over here," he explained.

"I see... do you have a few minutes? One of my coworkers interviewed you briefly last night and I wanted to go back and meet each of the interviewee's personally to go over their account of the evening. I see that you and the missus were out to dinner?" he said offering a manufactured smile.

"Yeah. I think my relationship with my wife is important, so I wanted to invest some time with her and thought it would be a good night to get a babysitter and take her out to dinner," the bishop responded very matter of fact.

"Where did you end up eating?" Winthrop asked. *And your dumb ass better not say Hooters, you lying sack of shit!*

"We ended up at the Olive Garden; it was a wonderful evening. I had the Fettuccine Alfredo, she had some herb-grilled salmon, and a bottle of Pinot Noir. Fantastic." the bishop said, impressing himself that he recalled the details of his dish, something for the detective to verify.

"So who got the fish?" Winthrop asked, stalling for as much time as possible.

"She did. I love the Alfredo," he said as the two laughed. *Yeah, that ain't all you love!*

Throughout the next hour Winthrop entertained the bishop in a rather in-depth interview regarding his deceased neighbor and how much he had come to know about the young lady. The bishop calmly answered each of the detective's questions, being extremely careful not to give too much information away that would implicate him in any manner or for any reason. He talked about how Gwendolyn moved into the complex about six months ago and knew from the nametag pinned on her uniform shirt that she must have been employed with a nearby Verizon Wireless store. The bishop even commented on how he invited her to attend his church, and for the past few weeks, she actually attended some of the services. Then he recalled how Gwendolyn found another church home and hung his head, disappointed in her new find- - or perhaps in his own shame.

"She was a sweet, young lady, always smiling, always so full of energy. What a shame. To think she was murdered," the bishop offered in condolence.

"We're working it the best we can right now; as soon as we hear something we'll let you know." Winthrop said.

The numerical page vibrated the detective's pager. Nonchalantly, Winthrop depressed the ever so small button, receiving the "10-42" signal. A basic ten-code used frequently by uniformed officers to signify to dispatch that they completed their tour of duty and were now going home, the code had been prearranged to be sent to Winthrop when the remainder of the homicide squad had accomplished their task and left the area.

"Sir, thank you for your time, it's been a pleasure meeting and talking with you. I'll let you get back to moving into your new apartment."

The bishop offered a wide, toothy smile and saw his guest out the front door. Just before completely closing the door, he scanned the parking lot looking for anybody or anything that appeared out of place.

While the expedition was somewhat fruitful, Winthrop wasn't satisfied with the minimal evidence recovered from the apartment. The detectives obtained everything they sought in the search warrant. Detective Gibson, who was quite handy with tools, quietly removed the toilet and cut away the drain trap in the piping in a matter of minutes. All ten fingertips were recovered as hoped, and each of the door knobs, particularly the exterior door knob to Gwendolyn's apartment, was swabbed. But now that Winthrop committed the bishop to a statement that he only knew 'Gwen' from casual passing and had never been to her apartment, Winthrop would have the bishop cornered if his DNA appeared on any of the swabs. However, asking for a DNA sample from the bishop would only tip his hand that investigators were closely looking at him as a suspect in her death. Most promising to the detective was the inadvertent statement made by the bishop during his interview.

"He was cool as a cucumber throughout the interview; I'm just hoping I didn't flinch when he said that it was 'a shame to think that she was murdered,'" Winthrop said, proudly grinning.

"Why's that?" Gibson asked not being privy to most of the information having just returned from a short getaway.

"Because we just found out today that she was murdered and haven't released it to the press. How the hell does he know she was murdered?" Winthrop said, looking over the top rim of his reading glasses.

"You've gotta love those Freudian slips," Gibson countered.

"Well, now that we know who the murderer is, how are we going to prove it?" Winthrop asked, awaiting any plausible suggestions.

****

The arrangements were complete. Mr. Anderson called the homicide office and reported his clients would be surrendering themselves to the authorities that day. Dave Winslow would be first at noon and Calvin Miller would appear at 2:00 p.m. Mr. Anderson assured the homicide detectives Dave would surrender the keys to the 2002 Mazda Protégé, and they could recover it at his father's business office where it was currently secured under lock and key. Mr. Anderson concluded the telephone call by ensuring the investigators they would receive 100% co-operation from his clients and their families.

Dave Winslow actually arrived just minutes before the plain bezel wall clock struck high noon his father and attorney accompanied him.

"As I promised, Dave Winslow is here to surrender himself. He does have a quick statement he would like to make here in my presence," Mr. Anderson said cuing his client.

Dave, whose head hung low as he walked into the precinct and waited to be taken into custody, raised his face in shame and said, "As directed by my counsel, I am electing to invoke my right to remain silent, am refusing to make any statements, and request my attorney be present during any questioning."

Well, there goes that opportunity.

The formality closed the door on the detectives who hoped after they secured Dave in the processing area, he would feel compelled to give investigators a full accounting of Calvin's transgressions. Now, with that hope evaporating right before their eyes, Dave carefully followed the direction of his attorney and invoked his Constitutional rights against self-incrimination.

"Also," Mr. Anderson said holding out a set of keys with the familiar Mazda logo dangling before the detective's eyes, "here are the keys to the Mazda Protégé as promised."

Jones took the keys and offered a professional gesture of gratitude for making the complicated matter rather simplistic.

"I must say," Mr. Anderson said, extending his hand for a final cordial handshake as their meeting reached its conclusion, "after having some time to speak with my client about these events surrounding his arrest, I'm not sure you have a solid case built against either him or Mr. Miller."

"As you are aware, Mr. Anderson, we usually don't seek an arrest warrant charging someone with murder without consulting with and getting the approval of the Chief Violent Crimes State's Attorney. Mrs. Collins has given us her complete blessing, intending to prosecute them both," Lang replied.

Giving one last tempered look at his father, Dave moved in front of the detectives, turned, and clasped his hands behind his back, awaiting the application of a set of handcuffs.

"No need for those today," Jones said, firmly placing his hand on Dave's shoulder. "We're only two doors away from the cellblock." As Dave was escorted behind the electronic steel door, he looked over his shoulder one last time to see his father hanging his head in humiliation, unable to take in the scene.

****

"I said I need a 9/16th wrench, not the ½ inch," Gibson said as he attempted to free the driver's seat from the floor mounts.

Lang and Jones walked into the crime lab garage wearing their best-worn jeans and t-shirts that could afford them the opportunity to play mechanic for a day.

"How far are we pulling this car apart?" Gibson quipped, his head now tucked under the dashboard with his legs protruding out from beneath the driver's door.

"As far as we need to," Jones answered. "With the twenty three carwash tokens and the car looking like it's been completely detailed, there's no way you can tell me that they got every drop of blood and mung off of this car that night. Something's gotta be left."

"If I remember correctly, Mike gave you an account that Austin was standing on the driver's side of the car when the shotgun went off, right," Gibson said.

"Yes," Jones and Lang agreed simultaneously.

"Then it would seem to me that we need to concentrate on pulling off the seals around the door jams and the windows; some blood had to have run down inside," Gibson reasoned.

Lang fetched a screwdriver and dismantled the interior panel from the driver's door. Systematically, the three detectives meticulously disassembled the driver's side of the Protégé, placing the dismantled parts on large sheets of brown paper torn from a spool and covering most of the concrete floor around the vehicle. Periodically, the team would stop, and with the assistance of the resident biologist, Lauren, the components would be sprayed with a luminal spray and the room darkened. Lauren ignited her flashlight, aimed her sight through the amber lens, and scanned the light particles for any evidence of bloodstains.

The light glided back and forth, across each of the saturated parts, searching for any evidence of a shimmering sparkle that resembled a blood drop or mung. After each item was inspected, it was sorted to a new location, giving the indication that was inspected and determined to be evidentially insignificant. As each part was moved from the 'to be examined' pile to the 'already examined' pile, concern grew within each of the detectives who knew how vital such evidence would be to bolster their criminal case. Perhaps Mr. Anderson's ill words regarding the status of their case were truer than they wanted to believe. The team weighed the possibilities as the distressing situation threatened the integrity of their case.

Turning on the lights in the garage, Lauren said, "That's it.

I've examined each piece, the door, the jams, the seals, the panels—nothing's illuminating, nothing. There's no blood."

"Come on, Lauren. This guy's chest was blown apart leaving a big ol' crater. There's gotta be something," Jones retorted.

"I'm telling you, Jones, I've looked. Unless you tear deeper into the car there's nothing more here to look at. Maybe we should call it a day," Lauren offered.

"'Call it a day, my ass!" Jones said indignantly. "What about all these windows? Did you see the dried yellow-tinged streaks running down them? What the hell is that? There's gotta be blood and shit mixed in with that!" he continued.

"You know, you might be on to something there Jonesy," Lauren said deep in thought. "If we can't find any DNA sources for the victim, we can still build a solid case, biologically speaking."

"What do you mean?" Lang asked, the group unanimously offering a perplexed look.

"Look. Take any employee's car off the front lot and we'll find DNA in it. We'll find DNA because most people don't take the time to thoroughly clean their cars on a daily basis. Skin cells should be flaking off on the steering wheel, gearshift, seat belt buckle, and all those other parts that you touch on a daily basis. I'm not finding that in this car, but I should be; this tells me that they went to extraordinary lengths to clean this car. You guys are absolutely right. Blood should have run down the windows, beneath the seals, and onto the components of the interior of the doors, but they didn't. So what if right after the shooting, they hit a nearby car wash and start cleaning this thing down really well, move it to another spot and clean it some more, then to another place and clean it again. With such extensive efforts in cleaning the car, they've removed the entire common DNA that we should be finding from where the owner uses the car daily. What I'm saying is it's not only unusual that we aren't finding the victim's DNA in such a violent murder, but it's also unusual we aren't finding the owner's DNA in the vehicle. Get it?"

"So if we shift our focus to show how unusually clean this

car is, maybe identify some of the varieties of chemicals used to clean it, we can show a jury the extreme efforts the suspects took to cover their trail," Lang reasoned.

"Exactly," Lauren said, gesturing her hand in agreement.

"Okay. So, where are the Q-tips?" Lang quipped.

****

After several weeks of turning over every possible clue and coming up empty handed, Winthrop's frustration was mounting, and it was beginning to show.

"You mother..." Winthrop shouted as he pitched the stack of criminal record checks across the room. "I know you did it .I know you killed that girl. You son of a bitch!" he seethed as his eyes searched his desktop for his most current notebook.

"How do you know *he* did it?" Lang asked the seething detective.

"I just know, something in my gut says he did it," Winthrop answered in a calmer voice.

"I'd stick with your gut," Lang replied. "They say that more so than not, you're gut instinct is always the right one!"

"And who the hell are *they*?"

"Beats me. But statistically speaking, *they're* right!"

Winthrop paused trying to sort the logic in the statement and then gathered the criminal records that had gone airborne minutes earlier.

"Nothing to go on?" Lang asked.

"Nope. Bone dry. I interviewed her entire family who can only give me names of two guys she's ever dated in her life. I chased them down and they had solid alibis. I subpoenaed her cell phone records and she didn't call anybody except mom and dad throughout the week and some of her girlfriends from church. She's squeaky clean. Jackass, on the other hand, seems to have done a great job cleaning up his trail 'cause I can't find it. His cell phone records confirm that he was at the Olive Garden when the fire broke out. It looks like he made some phone calls to some people around town and one guy down in Salisbury, but nothing that stands out."

"Salisbury?" Lang asked, recognizing that the town was at least a two-hour drive from the Baltimore metropolitan region. "Who lives down there?"

"I'm not sure yet. I'm waiting for the records to come back. As of now, I know who murdered Gwendolyn Morgan, but I can't prove it."

The room fell silent. Realizing that all investigative avenues were exhausted and knowing who murdered Gwendolyn was a familiar frustration for Cartwright and Lang as they, too, struggled with cases offering little, if any, evidence. As if a bad omen plagued the besieged detectives, each continued his struggle in search of evidence that would help them bring a successful resolution to their respective cases.

"When I get the cell phone records back from the Salisbury, Dude, I'll figure out my next step from there. Until then, I've exhausted everything."

In the days that followed, Verizon Wireless complied with the most recent subpoena requests, undoubtedly returned expeditiously due to the note attached to the cover sheet of the facsimile indicating the victim of this homicide investigation was a former employee of the company whose records may help bring justice for her mourning family. With freshly obtained records in hand, Winthrop sat quietly at his desk pouring through each line of information, occasionally referencing the Google Earth longitudinal and latitudinal software, searching out cell site information for the cell phones in question.

"Now we're talking. That's what I want to see," came the cry from the far corner of the office.

"What's that?" Lang asked.

"Remember how I said the bishop called someone in Salisbury?" Winthrop posed.

"Yeah."

"It turns out that he has a cousin who lives there and his cell phone left Salisbury, about two hours and fifteen minutes before the fire broke out. The nice thing is he must have talked on it the whole way up to Baltimore, 'cause I can see how they came up 50, then on 2, and around 695. In fact, the last call they make before heading back to Salisbury is to the bishop, and they're sitting right in the apartment complex. It was heading back only ten minutes after the 911 call came into the comm center. Now that's some good shit," Winthrop said pointing to the map on the computer screen. "Now it's time to stir the pot."

****

"Beth, the car came up clean. Cleaner than usual," Jones said, expressing some doubt about the case.

"But I still love the case. Anderson's an asshole. He's just trying to get you to doubt yourself. It's one of his favorite tactics," Collins advised. "Look, we've got the threatening phone calls, the cell tower information, and the shotgun. Then these two jackasses go on the run for two days before their attorney calls us to facilitate their surrender. If they didn't do anything wrong, why the hell did they surrender?" she said, sitting straight up in her leather chair. "They've filed a boatload of motions and we need to start preparing. From my preliminary talks with Anderson, he's already looking for an offer on the table. So here's my offer. Screw Miller! And I'll go with twenty years for Winslow."

"What's your goal with Miller?" Lang asked.

"Life. Though, he has a good argument that Miller acted in the heat of passion."

"Heat of passion? It isn't like Stacey was his wife and he found her in bed with someone else. This dude wanted Stacey for himself and killed the boyfriend to get him out of the way, though I'm not quite sure where the logic falls that Stacey will fall madly in love with him after killing Austin," Lang said abruptly.

"Love has led to many a murder," Collins said, cautiously shaking her finger. "Let's just focus on this one for now, please. I know life pans out to be about twenty years in Maryland, but for a first time violent offender with little if any criminal history to speak of, what else do you expect?" she asked.

"You don't think this would be a death penalty case?" Jones asked.

"Not at all. I know he drove across the county to chase down this boy and then shot him, but it just doesn't quite fit our guidelines," she explained, throwing her arm on the file in exasperation.

"Okay, so what if they don't plea?" Lang asked.

"Anderson wants to play some of his cards first. If he loses the motions, we take Miller to trial first. If Miller is convicted, Winslow will plea; otherwise both defendants could end up walking with a 'not guilty' verdict."

"Beth, if we go to trial, are you pulling the plea offer off of the table?" Lang asked.

"If we go to trial, yes, all bets are off," she said with a crooked smile.

CHAPTER NINE

"Damn it Commander! I don't give a rat's ass about what you think!" The sentiment echoed from down the corridor behind the closed wooden door. "All I know is I've got a dead girl and a viable suspect but no evidence to prove it! I know we've never tried it before! But we've got to do something!" Winthrop yelled as his face flushed red in near rage.

Raising his finger in an accusatory way, Commander Williams raised his voice. "Detective Winthrop. Let me remind you that you are a subordinate to me and as long as I'm in charge I—"

"Let me tell you something, Commander! I'm only required to respect the rank – there's nothing in rules and regs that says I've got to respect the idiot they promoted!" Winthrop quickly interjected, his blood pressure boiling. "You're always on our asses about solving these cases. Now that I have a way we can solve this case, you don't want to do it 'cause it might cost you too much money in overtime. So when you walk in the squad room and you see Gwendolyn Morgan's name up on the board still in green you can only blame yourself—and I don't want to hear any of your shit about these cases not getting solved," Winthrop shouted as he stormed out of the commander's office, slamming the door shut.

In just a few seconds, the same door flung open as the

short-statured commander tried to fill the doorway with an ominous presence that seemed laughable.

"Get back here, Winthrop! Get back here right now! I'm ordering you!"

Asshole! Winthrop grabbed his jacket and made his way out of the office.

****

When the bailiff called the courtroom to order, the two attorneys stationed themselves at their appropriate, richly-stained desks. Anderson had lugged in his folders, dropping them at their designated areas on the tabletop as Beth Collins called the matter before the court.

"Your Honor, at this time the State would like to call off the docket the cases of Calvin Miller and Randy Winslow." she said cuing the deputy sheriff's to bring in the two prisoners isolated from one another since their apprehensions.

Winslow was the first of the two prisoners escorted into the courtroom. Bound in jingling but obscured handcuffs and shackles, Winslow was positioned two seats away from counsel when the second defendant emerged from the back corner door, similarly bound, and was escorted to the chair immediately next to Mr. Anderson.

"Counsel, the files reflect Mr. Miller and Mr. Winslow have both been arraigned. The matter is now set before the court for the matter of motions. Is that correct?" the judge formerly inquired.

"Your Honor, that is correct," Mr. Anderson answered as he straightened the two folders lying close to the table's edge.

"Very well then, let's get on with it."

****

Loosening his tie and unbuttoning his top button, Winthrop felt the phone vibrating on his hip and retrieved the cell phone hoping that the caller ID would be any number other than the commander's. With some luck, Winthrop recognized it was his sergeant, Petrelli, who was trying to reach him.

"Hello!" Winthrop sharply greeted the Sergeant when answering the call.

"Hey, Keith. What happened earlier with the commander?" the Sergeant asked.

"Typical commander bullshit, if you ask me. We've exhausted everything in the Morgan case and he doesn't want to hear it, but he wants it solved. I threw out the idea about going up on a wire on the bishop's phone and he corked out 'cause of all the overtime that will generate, but you and I both know, little man will be on our asses first thing tomorrow morning about knowing who killed her, but not being able to solve it, I've had about enough, Sarge! It might be time for me to start looking for a new home," Winthrop said, somewhat calmer.

"So you want to go up on a wire?" Petrelli asked.

"You know, Sarge, I've spent twelve years in narcotics working wires and if anyone knows a case prime for a wire it would be me. We've tried everything else. What do we have to lose?" he challenged.

"I like the idea, and I don't think it's ever been done here in the history of the unit. Tomorrow you and I will sit down with the commander and see if we can iron all of this out. You know, he's pretty pissed at what you said," Petrelli said. "But I would have done the same thing. It's not about what the commander thinks or the overtime issues; it's about doing everything we can in these cases. It's about what the sign says hanging over the squad room door, Keith: 'We work for God!'"

****

The arguments proceeded logically, regimented, and in a sequence that brought Detective Jones to the stand to testify concerning the search of the first house that yielded the shotgun and duffel bag containing the shotgun rounds and 25mm cartridges.

"Detective Jones, you've just testified to the court that in the course of your investigation you learned that Mr. Miller and Mr. Winslow may have been staying at the new residence that Mr. Michael Winslow recently purchased and was renovating, is that correct?"

"Yes."

"And in your testimony, you indicated that you found a red and black duffel bag lying on Mr. Winslow's bedroom floor. Intrigued by what may be inside of that bag, did you, or did you not go into the bag and search for evidence pertaining to your investigation?" Anderson said as he painted a shrewd grin across his face.

"Yes, I went into the bag." Jones said.

"And did you have a search warrant for the house?"

"No. Mr. Michael Winslow gave us his consent to search." Jones felt his heart beginning to flutter as his chest grew hollow. *He's going to attack my search—and probably win. There goes the case!*

"What about the duffel bag? Did you get a search warrant for that?"

"I did not." Jones answered, regretfully knowing the road that this line of questioning was now taking.

"But you could have, couldn't have you? Gotten a search warrant for the gym bag?" Anderson asked.

"I didn't think that—"

"You didn't think that you needed a search warrant for the duffel bag, Detective?" Anderson charged, knowing that he was molding Detective Jones right in the palms of his hands. *Perhaps there is hope for the defendants in this case.* Anderson squared up to Jones who was now fidgeting in his seat. "It's a very simple legal principle that they teach you in the police academy, is it not, Detective Jones?"

"Yes, but—"

"But you had been up for many hours and you were tired. Instead of securing the duffel bag as evidence and obtaining a search warrant at a later date, as you're supposed to do, you elected to go ahead and search the bag, to take a shortcut. Didn't you?" Anderson asked pointedly.

"No, I didn't."

"You didn't do your job, Detective!" Anderson's sudden outburst startled everyone in the courtroom. With a deliberate stern tone, Anderson raised his voice and heighted his pace. "You have just sat here, under oath, and testified before the court that you obtained consent to search the house, but didn't obtain a search warrant for the closed duffel bag you found in the house when you knew the law required a search warrant for the duffel bag. Is that correct, Detective?" Anderson demanded.

"Yes," Jones said, realizing that he lost the battle.

"I have no further questions for this witness your Honor," Anderson said, glaring in joy at Jones.

****

The view from the tenth-floor corner office was spectacular. Luscious green landscape surrounded various suburban neighborhoods, reaching northward to rolling hills that graciously back-dropped the cityscape. As fresh sunrays streamed between the towering apartment buildings in the early morning hours, Winthrop and Petrelli entered the commander's office and shut the door.

"Good morning gentlemen," Williams said without any emotion. "Take a seat."

"Commander, we have two items of business that need to be addressed here this morning and I'd like to tackle the more important one first." Petrelli stated.

Laying his pen aside from jotting a quick note on his 'to do' list, Williams leaned back in his chair and prepared to listen to the apology he anticipated would be offered by Winthrop.

"First of all, Commander, the Morgan case has come to a point where we have exhausted every potential lead. Commander, we're at a dead end."

Williams slung forward in his chair, a little dismayed that his sergeant had evidently taken sides with his detective and had the audacity to consult him as to the matter of the Morgan investigation before offering an apology for Winthrop's intolerable conduct displayed the night before. Offering a perplexed look, Williams decided this time he would listen to his subordinate before offering any unsolicited outrage.

"Commander, Keith has exhausted every potential investigative avenue in this case. There are no fingerprints, no DNA, nothing to speak of forensically. Other than the arson detective's report that confirms an accelerant was placed in the bathroom, the point of origin for the fire, there's nothing else to go on. We have the card in the nightstand with the bishop's email address, and nothing else—nothing."

"Okay, so what's there left to do?" the commander asked coarsely.

"Well, Sir, I have a plan," Winthrop offered with a wry smile.

****

Aromas of delightful lentil soup, lightly seasoned artichokes with olive oil, and robust lamb pasta casserole made Alexander's Acropolis one of the favorite Greek restaurants in the area. Alexander, whose parents immigrated to the United States when he was only five years of age, remembered the motherland and was ardent about sharing his Greek heritage, especially the food, with all who entered the doors of his restaurant.

"Yahsu!" Alexander would say in his native tongue as he personally greeted each customer with a wide grin of appreciation before he escorted his customers to an awaiting bistro style table prepared with fine linen and silverware.

Having reached fifty-three years of age, Alexander never forgot the plight from which his family fled Greece as they sought a new beginning in this Land of Opportunity. Born on the outskirts of Larissa, Alexander would often recall the stark, snow-white covered Olympus Mountains that his father often drove past while making his way into town to find work. Alexander realized the work his father found must have been hard work, for he never forgot the feeling of the rough calloused hands that often supported him while sitting upon his lap late in the evening. He cherished such memories, particularly those as a child growing up in their diminutive four-room house. Alexander would often get lost in such reminiscing, acknowledging how fortunate and blessed he was to have been able to immigrate to the United States, get a good education, and become a successful businessman. It was no wonder Alexander was so benevolent with those in the community that surrounded him.

At precisely 9:00, just as it had been everyday, Alexander noticed Billy standing at the front door of his restaurant, his nose smashed against the glass, his right hand squared over his brow, blocking the sun's rays that were glaring in his eyes.

Alexander caught sight of the familiar figure peering into the front door as he put the finishing touches on the dinning room's place settings. He hurried over to the door, unlocked it, and greeted Billy with a firm pat on his back before re-locking the door behind them.

"Kaleemera, my good friend, Billy! How are you today?" Alexander asked with his usual warm greeting.

One of the less fortunate from the neighborhood, Alexander felt a great deal of compassion for Billy who was a Vietnam veteran, evicted from his apartment eighteen months ago and now homeless. Each day, Alexander would allow the veteran to come into the restaurant hours before opening and provide him a fine meal from the leftovers the day before.

Billy took his normal seat and stoically stared off into nothingness. His worn, leathered skin, twisted and knotted hair and reeking tattered clothes left a lot to be desired. However, Alexander saw something more.

"Billy, today I have a wonderful white bean soup and some broiled lamb chops you will certainly enjoy. Let me get Rodney to throw it together for you; it'll be out in just a few minutes," Alexander offered with a beaming smile before quickly returning to the kitchen and prompting Rodney to prepare the dish.

Billy sat motionless, continuing his sullen empty stare against the back wall as he waited for the only meal he would receive for the day. Hearing the dishes clank together in the far back reaches of the kitchen, two voices rumbled over one another; Billy's concentration strayed, as evidence of the verbal argument resonated from a closer distance.

****

"Because you were late again today, you are behind! And because you are behind, I will not be ready to open on time," Alexander sternly voiced to Rodney who was dicing the tomatoes for the numerous salad orders that would flood the kitchen by noontime.

Rodney looked up at Alexander with darting eyes. "You know what?" he said, fed up with the daily routine. "Everyday I come in here and have to prep all your food for lunch, but you start stacking all this other shit on me—mopping the floor, washing the dishes, and making that crazy guy something to eat when I'm supposed to be getting the food ready for lunch!"

"You don't like your job?" Alexander stepped forward, placing his hands on his hips. "You worked here before you were arrested, went away to jail for two years, and then you came back crawling to me looking for a job—and now you complain?"

"I'm tired of all your bullshit, yo!" Rodney exclaimed.

"Fine," Alexander exclaimed "you're fired! Now get your stuff, get out of my restaurant, and don't come crawling back to me looking for work; I will not rehire you."

Alexander turned and stormed off into the back office, taking a moment to reorient himself on the task of getting his restaurant opened in time for the lunch rush. Flipping through the Rolodex on the back edge of his desk, Alexander called a more trusted employee and pleaded his case, convincing him to come into work early and help with his dilemma. That task completed, Alexander returned to the kitchen, and after peering over the kitchen counter to see if Rodney left, saw Billy still patiently sitting at his table waiting for his meal. *Ah, poor Billy. I almost forgot.*

"I am so sorry, Billy," Alexander cried from behind the counter, "I'll have your food right out. Kids these days, always wanting something for nothing."

With great haste, Alexander slapped the piece of lamb onto the plate and slid it into the microwave. Pounding out "1:30" on the numeric keypad, he started warming the meat then focused on finding a bowl for the white bean soup. Ladling a healthy portion of the white bean soup into the bowl, Alexander darted to a second microwave, placed the bowl inside, tapping out the desired time to initiate the warming process. Grabbing a plastic cup from the dishwasher rack, he plunged it into the ice bin, scooped out some ice, and turned to the sink to fill the glass with chlorinated tap water.

"Billy," Alexander said as he made his way out from the kitchen, "My apologies that you—"

As he rounded the corner from the kitchen into the dining room, sudden, shearing pain radiated from the back of his neck down into the middle of his back. Rendering him motionless, he dropped the glass of iced water onto the hardwood flooring. In immutable shock, Alexander turned to see what suddenly immobilized him. Looking over his shoulder, Alexander saw the handle of the ten-inch butcher knife, plunged deep into his back, Rodney's hand firmly gripping the handle as his scowling face looked beyond the hilt, deep in Alexander's agonizing eyes.

"You can't fire me, I quit," he said giving the knife a hard twist, sinking the razor-sharp, cold steel deeper into Alexander's neck.

Alexander shrieked in horror as the last twist of the knife sliced through his carotid artery and his neck began spewing blood as if it were water spraying from an untamed garden hose. Sheer panic overtook the restaurant owner as he ran about the dining room, screaming, grabbing for the butcher knife still impaled in his back.

Upsetting tables, Rodney cleared a path, making his way to the front door. As he unlocked the door, he glanced back over his shoulder and watched as his former employer flailed in his suffering, then tore out the door.

****

Billy sat speechless, shaking with fear as terror transported him back to the 1968 Siege of Khe Sanh, where he and his fellow Marines, pinned down behind enemy lines, tenaciously fought off the Vietnamese in hand to hand combat. Seeing the knife lodged deep into Alexander's back rekindled images of a close friend whose nearly decapitated body had flopped about in the fierce and bloody skirmish. And just as it had occurred on the battlefield, Billy froze, watching in horror, wondering if he was next.

Alexander floundered his way back to the kitchen, grabbing the wall mounted phone off its receiver.

"911, what is your—"

"Help me! Help me!" he screeched into the phone.

"What's wrong, Sir?" the operator asked as the restaurant's name, address, and map coordinates automatically illuminated on her monitor.

"I've been stabbed! Help me! Help me! Rodney stabbed me," the shrilling voice pleaded.

The operator could tell the caller's situation was dire and had immediately forwarded the information to the police dispatcher in the first few seconds of the phone call.

"Who stabbed you, Sir?" she asked, trying to calm the caller.

"Help me! Help me!" he continued with his squealing pleas.

"Sir, I need you to calm down and tell me again, who stabbed you?" the operator asked encouraging the caller to give more information. But there was no response.

"Sir? Sir?" she called out.

Alexander, feeling cold and lethargic, lost the energy to scream and meandered unsteadily back out into the dining room. Using the disarrayed tables and chairs as support along the way, Alexander crept across the blood soaked floor until he reached the empty seat across from Billy. Alexander leaned forward, gripped the edge of Billy's table as blood poured from his wounds onto the pristine white tablecloth and dribbled onto the floor. Completely drained of all strength, Alexander slowly made his way into the black iron chair and leaned back. Looking deep into Billy's eyes, Alexander muttered a few garbled words before his lifeless body fell face forward onto the table as the last of his blood ebbed ever so slowly onto the floor beneath his feet.

His body trembled uncontrollably. Billy could only sit and stare at the dead man strewn across his table as the two microwaves signaled his meal was now ready.

CHAPTER TEN

As the marked patrol units swarmed onto the parking lot of Alexander's Acropolis, officers were able to ascertain some viable information from Billy, who stood nervously shaking out on the front sidewalk, blood spattered across his face and shirt.

"Mr. Johnson, I know you're upset, but you need to calm down and tell me what the guy looked like!" the officer demanded.

Unable to articulate his thoughts, the shell-shocked veteran could only utter a few cryptic phrases officers needed to decipher.

"Cook... black... that way," Billy babbled as he pointed to the rear of a strip mall located on the north side of the restaurant.

"Are you telling me the cook stabbed the owner?" the officer asked.

Billy could only stand and shake his head, making an affirmation as he wrapped his arms around himself seeking some level of security and comfort in the midst of his chaos.

"Dispatch," the officer said clicking his lapel mic. "According to a witness, the suspect is the cook, possibly African-American, and was last seen fleeing on foot behind the shopping center located on the north side of our location. Can you see if you have 'air' on the channel?"

The request for the aviation unit was broadcasted countywide over the police frequencies and brought 'Boomer' onto the channel.

"Air One is on the channel dispatch. What do you have?"

"Air, we have a stabbing that just occurred. Wanted is a subject, possibly African-American, fleeing on foot behind the shopping plaza north from the Acropolis restaurant. The suspect was described to be the cook, so we're not sure on a clothing description and are guessing he may be wearing a white or white and black cook uniform," she advised. "We're having a hard time sorting through the information with this witness," she further explained.

"10-4, we're en route. Let me know when we have something better on the clothing."

"Air, I'm direct," the dispatcher said as her fingers chattered against the console's keyboard.

It was only a matter of minutes before the helicopter eliminated the expanse between the airport and the west side of the county, swooping down to a lower altitude, and circling overhead. Orienting themselves with the immediate area of the restaurant, Air One shot up to a higher platform and broadened his circular searching pattern.

"Air One dispatch, can you check with the units and see if any one has been in the woods behind that shopping plaza?" the aviator requested.

"Air, units are just arriving on the scene and we're still setting up a perimeter." The dispatcher explained.

"Okay, dispatch," he responded. "Let me check the area and... wait a minute, dispatch! Start me some units up to the access road along the power lines next to the wooded area. I have a black male, wearing a white shirt and black pants, running eastbound along the access road."

The sudden announcement caused a number of patrol units to scurry from their current searching parameter, making haste as they came in from three different egresses with the intentions of surrounding the fleeing suspect and stopping him dead in his tracks.

"Okay 3-Baker-11," the aviation officer said giving

direction from above, "he's running right towards you. When he rounds that corner he's gonna know you're there."

Instinctively the officer pulled his sidearm from its secured holster. With a firm two-handed grip, he pressed it forward in anticipation of the target that would find his way into his sights.

"Hands up, get on the ground, asshole! Do it now or I'll shoot!" the officer commanded while centering the kitchen-clad torso into his dulled iron gun sights.

The worn down sprinter glimpsed into the wood line to his left, seeing the figures of two uniformed officers, one armed with an M16 rifle, darting through the woods directly towards him. A quick glance to his right revealed three uniformed officers descending the hill, also having him bracketed in their gun sights. From the rear, he could hear the seething German shepherd bearing down on his position, the distant barking growing closer with each passing second. It was pointless, fleeing would cause certain chase by the K9, if not by being riddled with bullets flying from a multitude of directions. With all avenues of escape closed, Rodney raised his hands, interlaced his fingers atop his head, and dropped to his knees.

"Air One, dispatch," the radio transmission erupted from the Eurocopter hovering overhead, "Subject is in custody!"

****

It was a brilliant plan. All of the ground work was laid in preparation for this one important, decisive moment when Gwendolyn Morgan's murderer would either take the bait or go free despite the careful watch of the weary detectives who had overturned every possible lead in the investigation, coming up empty handed.

Each cubical allowed just enough room for the desktop computer, a notepad, and a set of tattered headphones tethered to a small component box giving the user easy access to adjust the volume while monitoring the phone calls. Getting permission to use such tactics was no easy task. Winthrop, accustomed to such investigative techniques when working in the Vice/Narcotics Unit years ago, tackled the daunting legal obligations required before securing the Title III wiretap order. The application in and of itself measured 137 pages in length, describing to the judge the nature of the criminal investigation, the investigative techniques employed, the information learned from each of those efforts, and how the Title III wiretap order would benefit the investigation. It was familiar territory to Winthrop, being able to justify to the fullest degree, the legal requirements demanded by any judge. Such an intrusion was regarded as a deep infringement upon one's individual rights. Just cause would be the only requirement, but if approved, the entire process would be set to certain time constraints and closely monitored by the State Attorney's Office and the judge himself. A detective with Winthrop's experience only ensured that the entire process would be carried out within full compliance of the law and give investigators an honest chance to develop the scanty case already set against the bishop.

"It's been weeks since the murder," Winthrop announced to the group of detectives and attorneys gathered for the initial briefing. "Murph tells me that the three cubicles will be set up by the end of the day and we should be online with the three phone numbers by 9:00 tonight. We'll monitor the lines for three days and make sure everything is in good working order. Once we're satisfied, then we'll stir the pot!"

"What three lines are we up on?" asked one of the attorneys who had become acquainted with the case hours earlier.

"We're up on the bishop's home phone, cell phone, and his wife's phone, just to see if she suspects any infidelity," Winthrop replied. "We've already been out to speak with him on several occasions about the case during the past few weeks. Now that everything has quieted down, it's likely that over the next few days there won't be any conversations about the murder," he said, standing at the head of the conference table holding the officially signed copy of the order. "This is the first wiretap we have ever done in the history of this unit, so minimizing calls that are privileged under the law is vitally important. Does anyone have any questions?"

For most, the process was routine. And while the formalities of being briefed about the case gave little more insight than everyone already had about the case, the briefing was relatively short and sweet, leaving everyone involved anxious to make their contribution to ensnare this perverted killer.

As predicted, the three phone lines were up and running in the designated cubby-hole with a detective monitoring the lines around the clock. At 6:00 p.m., Detective Carlos Sanchez entered the monitoring room, lugging his latest library find, a historical account of Jack the Ripper, and his bed pillow. With calls dying off after 2:00 a.m., his sweatpants and t-shirt combo made for comfortable attire while sleepily monitoring the low drummed hisses throughout the midnight shift. As he prepared to relieve the detective already posted on station number two, Sanchez anticipated a restful and relaxing overnight twelve-hour shift. Tossing his bed pillow into the chair and the book onto the back corner of the minuscule desk, Sanchez placed the headphones on his ears and maneuvered the mouse about the screen. *Looks like everything is in order, not much activity. Good!* Sanchez fluffed his pillow, reclined, and closed his eyes.

****

Detectives stood in the monitoring room, watching their suspect evaluate the restraints that had him firmly secured to the wall in the second interview room. Slinging his cuffed hand back and forth, Rodney thought back to earlier in the day when he was preparing food, never imagining he would find himself answering for taking the life of another human being. The situation, he knew, would change his life forever.

Stanton and Lang entered the room. Dropping his notepad onto the desk, Stanton reached into his pants pocket, retrieved his keys, and uncuffed Rodney from the wall. Rodney, still chained with leg irons, coupled his hand around his wrist, rubbing away the grooves the metal restraints left.

Having already collected his blood-stained clothing and securing a statement from the sole eyewitness, Stanton didn't feel the necessity to belabor the process. Getting straight to the point would surely convey to Rodney the investigators really didn't need to waste their time with a statement from a cold-blooded murderer. It was Stanton's intentions to jump this hurdle, get him off to his bail hearing, and tidy up the bundle of paperwork that the State Attorney's Office would require in the next few days to initiate the official grand jury proceedings.

"All right, Rodney, we all know why we're here and…"

****

Three grueling days of listening to uneventful phone calls to and from the bishop left every detective dreading their turn at the drudgery. With the telephone lines usually connecting between the bishop and his mother, the frequency of the conversation typically reached a crescendo when his mother would ask, "Is there anything new going on?" which often followed with the anticipated, "Nope" answer that would ultimately ensue with a segment of uncomfortable silence between the two parties. *Yes, the low drum hiss.* Not that any of the detectives pulling the long twelve-hour shifts would expect the bishop to give an explicitly detailed account of the brutal murder as an updated happening of the day. But, one slip of the tongue could propel investigators into a whole new direction that could potentially yield some evidentiary information and shore up this case.

Winthrop entered the secured room, tossing his dress coat and attaché folder onto an unoccupied chair.

"Anything going on?" Winthrop asked.

"Nope," replied a detective with a grin on his face, "nothing—same ol' shit, different day."

"Well, that's about to change," announced Winthrop. "You boys need to get ready, we're gonna put a fire under the bishop's ass tonight—wait 'til you see this!"

****

Southwest Airlines Flight 731 made its final approach

109

towards runway number 17L at Orlando International Airport, touching down at 8:06 p.m. Simply carrying a small tattered brown leather briefcase, the two detectives made their way off the airplane and straight to the rental car counter to initiate their mission. Wasting no time, the two detectives were well aware they needed to cover 32 miles in 45 minutes, conduct their interview, and return to the airport in time to catch their 11:27 p.m. redeye flight back home to Baltimore.

Securing a brand new Pontiac Grand Prix, the detectives installed their GPS and navigated to Florida State route 408, heading in a northeasterly direction towards their objective. Finding routes 408 and 417 relatively clear this time at night, they made good time and pulled up to the curb in front of the address: a small flamingo pink bungalow in desperate need of maintenance and renovations.

Straightening his tie and squaring his jacket, Jones stepped out of the car with Stanton just a few paces behind. Both noticed how dark the location was as they approached the porch and offered a hard, firm knock on the dilapidated wooden door. Anticipation grew in both of the detectives as they wondered if their journey would be in vain, or if perchance, they would be required to spend the night without having the opportunity to pack for the occasion.

"Who is it?" asked a faint elderly voice from deep within.

"It's the police department," Jones answered, shooting a crooked smile at Stanton. *We didn't say which police department.*

The locking mechanism clattered and the door creaked open, the delicate older woman sticking her face between the door's crevices to see who was bothering her at this late hour.

"Mrs. Woodridge? May we have a moment of your time?" Jones asked displaying his credentials.

"May I ask what this is about?" Mrs. Woodridge asked.

"Yes, ma'am. We're investigating the murder of a Gwendolyn Morgan and your son, James Woodridge, is our main suspect..."

****

At precisely 9:37 p.m. the computer chirped to life, announcing an incoming phone call to the bishop's cell phone. The caller ID confirmed his mother was calling.

"Hello," the bishop said groggily, awaking from a short nap.

"James, honey? You aren't going to believe this, but I just had two visitors here at the house!"

"Oh, yeah," he said, wiping his hand across his face in a meager attempt to become fully conscious.

"Two homicide detectives from Maryland. Do you know what they told me?"

The bishop's eyes shot wide open, his heart nearly pounding through his chest. "No, what?" he said sitting straight up on the edge of the bed.

"They told me you killed that girl who lives above you, and they have evidence to prove it. They're just waiting for the State's Attorney to sign off on the paperwork. They'll be getting a warrant for your arrest. James, honey, they gonna charge you with first degree murder! James, what is going on?"

Stunned at the news, shear silence overwhelmed the bishop and left him unable to formulate any logical response to the startling revelation.

"Who is it?" the bishop's wife asked, as she now stirred from her sleep next to her husband.

Feeling as if he was cornered, the bishop gave a darting look towards his wife. As his mind crazily sought for a response to offer to his concerned mother, he walked out from the bedroom onto the apartment balcony.

"Mom, they ain't got nothing on me. They're only targeting me 'cause I live downstairs and they have nothing else to go on. You sayin' they're trying to pin this on me?"

"James, from what they told me it sounds like you may have done it, They say they have Internet records where you were emailing her on a daily basis and they know you raped and killed her. James, please tell me you didn't do that! Please, James," Mrs. Woodridge pleaded.

The bishop dropped his head and rubbed the tears away that were forming from his recollection of the scene. He recalled how beautiful Gwendolyn was; her petite stature and shapely figure were irresistible. *How'd they get my email?* he pondered in his stillness.

"James, you're supposed to be a man of God! You're supposed to be married and an assistant pastor in the church. Why were you emailing this young, single girl?"

"Mom, I swear over Dad's grave, I only sent her emails about events at our church. Nothing inappropriate ever happened. You know I'm a faithful husband and father, I would never do anything like that. Them detectives are trying to pin this on me 'cuz they can't find the real killer. That's all. You'll see. If they charge me, I'll beat it in court."

"Okay James, I hope you're right. But they seemed pretty convincing."

****

The small group of detectives gathered around the one monitoring station and listened to the conversation in its entirety through the external speakers.

"Well, the next few minutes will determine if the cost for the plane tickets and rental car were worth the investment," Sergeant Petrelli said as the detectives huddled, anxiously waiting for the next phone call. Surely the news must have rattled the bishop's cage. He would have to reach out to someone and talk about his legal predicament.

Two minutes hadn't quite passed when the computer chirp alerted the investigators that the bishop's cell phone was now making an outgoing phone call to a landline in Salisbury, Maryland.

"Who the hell does he know on the eastern shore?" one investigator asked.

"He's got some cousins that live there. Somebody jump on that number and start running it down," Petrelli ordered.

After two detectives each copied the phone number off the glaring computer screen, they scrambled to two separate computer stations, entering the necessary information to begin tracking the phone number. As the remainder of the squad stood around the console, the audio clicked over on the monitoring speakers as the unknown number picked up the bishop's call.

"Yo! What's up?"

"Nothing much. What's going on down there?" the Bishop asked.

"Nothing man, why you calling so late?"

"Just checking in, making sure everything was all right down there."

"Well, if you're calling me out of the blue, everything ain't all right now is it? They leaning on you?"

"Watch what you say, they may be tracing the calls."

"Got it. So what do you want?"

"Just calling to see if there's been anything going on down there, that's all," the bishop said.

"Like I said, nothing's going on. We're all cool down here."

"Okay, I just need to check on one more thing. You get rid of everything?"

"Thought you said to watch what we say," the unknown voice scolded. "Like I said, everything is cool down here."

****

"That's it!" Winthrop yelled at the monitor. "I've got you now, you son of a bitch! And I've got you by the balls."

Dashing for his jacket and attaché case, Winthrop and Gibson darted for the car.

"Where are we going?" Gibson asked.

"Salisbury, we've got some interviews to do!"

CHAPTER ELEVEN

The drive down to the Eastern Shore was usually a scenic venture as the example of level fields sown with soybeans or corn transcended into sandy dunes and causeways nearing the shoreline. However, at 11:00 at night, there would be little scenery for the two detectives to take in during their car ride. With few troopers stationed in the median monitoring the traffic at this late hour, US-50 proved to be a quiet ride for the flat foots racing to get to their target before the situation took any sudden turns.

Three patrol officers and a sergeant gathered at the station in anticipation for their guests who would be arriving any minute. As Officer Crawford, a third generation police officer, finished assembling his contacts report, Winthrop and Gibson bounded into the lobby, and were swept behind the secured door into the squad room.

"I'm just finishing this report for you," Crawford said as the last few pages spat out of the printer.

"I appreciate you guys helping us out with this. We're pretty convinced that this guy will be the key to breaking this case—providing that he talks, of course," Winthrop said cracking a smile.

"When you called us, we jumped right on it and started running down as much information as possible. Looks like that hard-line number comes back to a Vernon Giles of 312 Union Street; he's a local dealer and has family up in Baltimore. When we ran his criminal record, we found he has a warrant out for his arrest for a failure to appear in court last month on some traffic charges. So we went over and locked him up; he's in the back."

Winthrop grinned with approval. *You gotta love it when they make it that easy for you.* "When can we talk to him?"

The room, like most other police interrogation rooms, sported little if any furniture and fixtures. Vernon Giles sat handcuffed at the side of a large metal desk that only offered one additional chair where the booking officer took some comfort in the age-old facility while completing the booking process.

The metal door unexpectedly swung open rousing Vernon from his slumber, surprisingly seeing two detectives in suits standing before him. Regaining some of his senses, Vernon raised an eyebrow and asked why two detectives were in the room.

"That's pretty simple, Vernon. You're in a shitload of trouble, and we're here to help," Winthrop said grinning as he sparked up a cigarette.

Winthrop settled into the chair where the booking officer was sitting just moments ago as Gibson slid in a chair behind him before slamming the door shut to the desolate and homely looking room.

"Let's see, two detectives' in suits—my guess is you're from Baltimore," Vernon said rather cocky.

"Good guess," said Winthrop. "Looks like today's your lucky day."

"How's that?" Vernon asked, raising his cuffed hand in front of the detectives as a reminder of his plight.

"You're not going to have to worry about this FTA warrant," Winthrop said.

"Why do you say that?" Vernon asked as Winthrop drew in a long drag on his cigarette.

"Cause after I charge you with first degree murder," Winthrop said exhaling a puff of smoke directly into Vernon's face "an FTA warrant will be the last thing you'll be worried about!"

Vernon immediately knew that a snare had sprung as his mind raced with the various scenarios that brought him to this point. Was it the phone call earlier from the bishop that led to tonight's arrest? If so, what did the bishop say to the detectives to make them think that he was responsible? Vernon stared hard at the floor while searching his mind for the most likely and probable solution, but his reasoning failed as he wrangled in his sea of possibilities. Not sure what to say, Vernon looked up at the detectives and decided to call their bluff.

"I don't know what you're talking about," he uttered half-heartedly.

Winthrop and Gibson looked at each other and grinned. Vernon elected to make the night a long one where he would have to be convinced the detectives secured enough information to secure a life-long conviction.

"Oh, so you don't know anything about a young lady who was murdered upstairs from James' apartment and the fire that happened shortly thereafter?" A smirk drew across Winthrop's face.

"Nope," Vernon said trying to offer his best poker face, "I don't know anything about it."

"Really, looks like things could get real ugly for you in a courtroom setting when we put your cell phone records up on the screen and show the jury all the telephone calls you made to James that night. What will be really cool is when we put up the map overlay that will show you driving from Salisbury to Baltimore and back to Salisbury the night of the fire. Sticking with the 'I don't know what you're talking about' story will guarantee an easy conviction for you. And with this being such a brutal murder, Vernon, who's to say when you'll get out of jail."

Winthrop adjusted his chair, leaning in close to Vernon's face. As the beads of sweat ran down Vernon's forehead, Winthrop ever so softly whispered, "Like I said, Vernon, today's you're lucky day. You can be a witness and tell me about what really happened, or you can stick with your 'I don't know' bullshit and make yourself a suspect—giving me the pleasure of ramming this first degree murder charge straight up your ass. It's your choice Vernon; what's it gonna be?"

Sweat poured from Vernon's brow as he contemplated his options. He had already served time in jail on a number of drug offenses and the last one landed him a solid three years before he was able to get back out on the street. Jail, he knew, was a place he didn't want to be. As if looking at a hand of cards, Vernon thought carefully, and decided he should explore his options a little further before making a decision.

"You can't charge me with murder. I didn't kill anyone," Vernon sneered.

"What kind of jailhouse lawyer bullshit is this?" Winthrop demanded. "Haven't you heard of accessory before or after the fact?"

Vernon's confidence suddenly erased from his face and was replaced with a new and genuine fear. He heard this legal jargon on many occasions when discussing charges with cellmates in local jail systems. He also knew in the State of Maryland anyone charged as an accessory in any felony crime was also charged as if they were the principle actor in that crime. His blood turned cold as he decided that he'd made an irrational move and may have just pushed the detective over the edge.

"Let me tell you something, Vernon. I ain't here for the bullshit. You can either be a witness or you can be a suspect, the choice is yours. But if you decide that you want to be a witness, then you better speak up and lay it all down like it happened or I'm charging you with the murder!" Winthrop screamed at the prisoner.

Vernon sat motionless as the reality of the moment sank in deep. As much as he could determine, he was out of options. *If I tell them what happened, they charge me. If I don't tell them what happened, they charge me. Either way, I'm screwed!*

His head dropped in sudden surrender. Vernon glanced up, and with all expressions washed away from his face and asked Winthrop "Can I have a cigarette?"

****

Early rain clouds that showered a soft gentle drizzle over the sleeping community masked dawn's morning light. All was quiet as the couple rested comfortably in the warmth from each other's bodies, peacefully lying next to one another on the fine silk linens.

The abrupt slamming of the front door caused the wife to sit straight up in bed, pulling up the linen to cover her breasts from the uninvited intrusion. As the front door flew open and crashed into the wall, the husband mustered his senses. Realizing that his home was being overrun, the man of the house rolled over onto his stomach, reaching over to the top drawer of the nightstand and sliding open the drawer. He reached in and fished for the .40 caliber pistol he always kept prepared for such an occasion. But, before he could secure his defense, a dark figure loomed over his bed pressing hard cold steel into the husband's temple.

"Get your hands where I can see them!" the dark ominous figure commanded.

Considering whether he could find his Beretta and get off a round, he hesitated. But when he heard the familiar click of the hammer pulled back on the gun pressed against his head, the husband reconsidered and slowly withdrew his empty hand from the nightstand. Offering both hands into the air to show that he was not armed and was compliant, a second dark figure grabbed his wrist and wrenched his arm behind his back. He could hear the ratcheting of the cold metal restraints and feel them clamping as they were applied to both wrists and secured behind his back.

"James Woodridge," the dark figure stated, "you're under arrest."

"For what?" came the objectionable tone from the missus.

"The murder of Gwendolyn Morgan."

****

James sat frozen in the chair of the interview room, mulling over what would happen to him in the next few hours. *They couldn't have developed enough evidence to find me guilty beyond a reasonable doubt!* He inspected his wrist tethered to the steel pipe bolted to the floor.

Winthrop opened the door and poked his head into the interview room, "James, you want something to drink or a snack before we get started?"

"The only thing I need is an attorney," the bishop replied.

"Are you invoking your rights and asking for an attorney?" Winthrop asked, surprised at the sudden legal assertion, knowing his door of opportunity to secure a confession just evaporated.

"Yes! 'Cause I didn't do nothing!"

"You didn't do nothing? You didn't do nothing?" Winthrop repeated sarcastically a second time. "Let me tell you something, Champ: we got a whole lot of shit on you. Try this on for size: We found the 'thinking of you card' you sent her with your email address on it. We subpoenaed those records and got the messages you emailed her."

"No you didn't."

"Does 'I'd like to get to know you better' sound familiar, Jackass?" Winthrop retorted.

The bishop sat attentively listening as the detective's recitation of the chronological events that unfolded in the investigation spilled forth.

"So we got your phone records and know who you've been calling."

"That doesn't prove nothing!"

"No? But it does prove that on the night before the fire, and again while you were *conveniently* out on a date with your wife, that you called this dude—um let's see, what's his name? Ah yes, Vernon, Vernon Giles—some cousin of yours from Salisbury, Maryland."

"So I have family, big deal! What's that prove?"

"The fact that you're related to Vernon Giles proves nothing. But, the fact that Vernon Giles has agreed to proffer with the State's Attorney and give a full and accurate account of the murder, describing how he set the fire—now that's a whole different story."

The bishop was speechless. His countenance fell.

"And you call yourself a man of God," Winthrop charged. "Wait until your congregation hears about what you've done and sees you convicted in court and whisked off to jail for the rest of your natural life. Hey, you know what, maybe you can start a prison ministry," the detective cracked.

"Vernon didn't tell you anything!" he countered.

"Oh yeah? Wanna bet?" said Winthrop.

"Vernon didn't tell you nothing," the Bishop said. "You're just trying to get me to say something, trip me up on my words."

Winthrop, who was standing during this entire confrontation, pulled up a chair, and rolled right up in front of the bishop. Pulling his head back, the bishop offered a scowl across his face, reinforcing his disbelief in Winthrop's purported conjecture.

"Do you know when I talked to Vernon?"

The bishop only offered an empty blank stare as his response.

"Right after your mama called you about the two detectives paying her that little surprise visit..."

The bishop continued his haughty stare.

"Want to know how I know that?" Winthrop asked leaning even further into the bishop's personal space. "We were on a wire and we were listening. Mama's not too sure you're telling the truth. Problem is, you called Vernon right after talking to Mama, remember that, Pastor Woodridge? Do you remember that phone call?"

The bishop's mind flipped back to the phone call just the day prior. *What exactly did I say?* He couldn't have said anything incriminating. Uncomfortable with the calm cool detective in his face, the bishop continued to stare him down refusing to offer any answers, eliminating any potential of his words being turned against him in a court of law. He decided he would simply sit and listen to the detective to see whether or not he had done his job and assembled a case that would be worthy of pursuing such legal actions.

"Do you remember that call?" Winthrop repeated. "'Cause if you don't it really doesn't much matter, we have it recorded," Winthrop said, offering a sinister smile. "Remember? You called Vernon and asked if anything was going on. He asked if *they* were leaning on you, *they* being the police. Remember James? And then you warned him to be careful about what was said because you thought we were tracing the calls. Good job, James. Not only were we tracing them, but we had a valid court order to record them. And then you make your bonehead mistake. But that's okay, even assholes are entitled to a few bonehead mistakes. Do you remember your bonehead mistake, James? Do you?"

James' memory came rushing back ever so clear; his mind brought to that moment in the conversation when his need to know overpowered his discipline to keep from talking about the matter on a potentially compromised telephone line. He didn't feel secure at the moment and was concerned that this undone task would unravel the mastery of performing the perfect crime. Who would know? Who could say? James thought through the series of events and realized his urgency to feel secure may in fact lead to his downfall. Understanding the detective was about to impart that very flaw to him, the bishop broke his trained eye away from Winthrop's and gazed upon the far back wall.

Almost as if they were playing a game of poker, Winthrop saw the bishop break his stare and knew the bishop realized he was holding a losing hand—not that he could use the statement in a formal court proceeding as evidence. Winthrop continued with his banter just as a matter of principle. After all, someone needed to speak on behalf of Gwendolyn.

"You do remember, don't you Pastor Woodridge?" Winthrop said, causing the bishop to break his concentration and give the detective a darting look before resuming his stare against the blank back wall.

"You remember it all. How lovely she was; how much you wanted her. She was a beautiful prize, wasn't she, Pastor? Every curve on her brick-house body calling out to you each time she walked up those stairs. No doubt you were probably looking out your window, watching her without her knowledge, gazing through the peep hole just to get a glimpse of that tight ass as it walked by your door and up the stairs. It was too much for you, wasn't it?" Winthrop softened his voice even more, "Then you decided to make your move. Send her a card. Tell her she had a secret admirer. Give yourself time to woo her over."

The bishop sat absolutely still, listening to every word that fell off the detective's lips. He recalled those earlier passionate days when his lust raged uncontrollably, and he longed to have this forbidden fruit. Now he concentrated on not moving, not giving any indication to the detective that his recounting of the events was tearing him apart inside.

"You couldn't bear it any more, could you? You finally had to have her. So you went upstairs but found yourself hesitating before you knocked on her door. It was like being back in high school and getting ready to ask the most beautiful girl in the school out on a date. You knocked, she answered, and you stumbled over your words, but you finally get it out that you are the face behind the pj356@iemail.com. She's disappointed and goes to close the door, but you force your way in. You want to convince her that you're in love with her and everything will be perfect. But she wants nothing of it, nothing to do with you." Winthrop continued in the slightest of a whisper, "Then you snap, you grab her, drag her down the hallway, and throw her on the bed. She fights back, but she's no match for you, and as you climb on top of her she begins to scream…"

The bishop could feel his heart racing a hundred miles an hour, as if it would explode from his chest any minute. In spite of the cooler temperature in the compact room, sweat poured down the bishop's forehead, dripping onto the front of his yellow button down short sleeve shirt. Winthrop knew he had the bishop exactly where he wanted him. But with the bishop straining to maintain focus on the back wall, he determined not to make any indication that the investigator was having any affect upon him.

"…so you wrap your hands around her throat and squeeze

until the screaming stops. But it doesn't end there, does it James? No," he said shaking his head, "you have your way with her and then when you're finished, you come to your senses and realize your beautiful prize is dead. 'Oh, no! What do I do?' Your mind begins to race… 'I've got to clean her off or they'll get my DNA!' So you strip her completely nude, carry her into the bathroom, and wash her down. That's when you start feeling the burning sensation of the scratches on your body from where her fingernails were digging deep into your skin as she was starving for breath. Thinking about the skin cells we'd find under her fingernails, you get a knife, cut off her fingertips, and flush them down the toilet."

Winthrop sat back to let the facts sink deep within the bishop's intellect, allowing him a brief moment to ponder over the revelations disclosed to him. Knowing he now had the upper hand, Winthrop relaxed comfortably in his chair and continued his discourse.

"We've got her fingertips, James," Winthrop said with all calculation.

The bishop's head snapped directly towards Winthrop, making immediate eye contact, revealing the horror tormenting him within.

"Oh, yes… and we're scraping her fingernails right now, James, looking for any foreign DNA that may have been left behind."

The bishop slowly turned his head away from the detective, resumed his empty stare, and fought with every fiber of his being to keep his emotions in check.

"Then you realized you probably haven't didn't do a thorough job cleaning up from your little crime spree, so, you call up Vernon and ask him for a favor. A date and time are set and you know it is important that you're not there at the scene when the fire breaks out, so you create a strong alibi that turns our eyes of suspicion off of you, onto someone else."

Winthrop leaned back in towards the bishop with a sharp grin, "But you didn't count on Vernon getting identified, breaking down, and telling us the whole story, did you, James? Vernon told us about the phone, the drive up from the Eastern

Shore, the BP station where he bought the gas can and gasoline, how he went into the apartment, doused the bathroom floor, and set the place ablaze. You didn't expect him to tell us about how he singed the hair off his hands before fleeing the apartment. And you sure didn't expect him to tell us how he threw everything away in the trash dumpster at the Methodist Church around the corner from his house."

This revelation caused another darting glare by the bishop who was now convinced Vernon revealed all he had known in an effort to save his own skin. *There is no honor among thieves or family.*

"Let me ask you one question, James. How does it feel to know you have shed innocent blood?"

The question was more than the bishop could bear. Unable to hold back the tears from the accurate and vivid recounting of his sins, they freely flowed down his face.

"If you didn't do anything," Winthrop asked, "tell me this: Why are those tears running down your cheek?"

CHAPTER TWELVE

Traffic was brutal on that bright and cool spring morning. Even after the three-car fender bender moved to the shoulder of the northbound interstate corridor, the rubberneckers slowing down to take in the scene gridlocked that section of highway for hours.

Charles rounded the corner and pulled into the Walcott Financial Group parking lot. Punching the accelerator in an effort to shave off a few seconds, Charles' silver Audi A4 convertible came to an abrupt stop in his assigned parking space near the rear entrance to the three-story office building complex. Leaving the ragtop down, he grabbed his lunch cooler and casually navigated his way to the rear entrance, entering into the musty stairwell, and scaling the concrete tiled steps to his second floor office.

Despite the aggravation of the routine traffic patterns, Charles' day began as he expected. A manager of the mortgage department in the Walcott Financial Group, Charles' team had recently experienced leaps and bound in their profit margin necessitating many of the employees to come into the office under the cover of the early morning darkness, just to ease the pace of the refinancing applications waiting to be processed. As Charles ambled past the maroon woven cubicles, he could hear the resonating sounds of computer keyboards feverishly chattering and the oversized coffee peculator gurgling in its last efforts at creating the morning's dark roast. His office key ready, Charles made the last turn towards his private office door to find it already standing open.

"Good morning, Charles," bellowed the voice from within.

Charles' heart sunk deep into his chest as he realized that Mr. Kozlov, his manager, arrived on time for the morning meeting that had slipped his mind.

"Working banker's hours today are we?" Nicholae asked.

"Mr. Kozlov, I'm sorry, but traffic was gridlocked and—"

"Yes, yes, yes, I've heard it all before," Nicholae said, waving his hand about wanting to speak about more important matters. "Where do we stand on the Brady account?"

Charles immediately recognized the problem. He obviously hadn't had the opportunity to be briefed when he arrived at the office, and with life weighing heavy on his mind lately, he didn't have the foresight to call the loan officer handling the case and get the necessary information. In yet another failure, he was not prepared, nor did he have the expected information, which set the unrelenting Mr. Kozlov into a frenzy.

"Charles," Mr. Kozlov said, "you've been dropping the ball a lot lately. Perhaps I should consider finding a more competent manager!"

Mr. Kozlov stormed out of the office, leaving Charles in his wake, unable to muster the dignity to raise his head. With a shrug of his shoulders as mere gesture of blithe, Charles circled around his desk, plopped himself in his chair, shook his mouse, and watched the computer monitor come to life.

****

His eyes darted back and forth between the case folders strewn across the defense table as Calvin Miller carefully thought through each of the components of the investigation and the detailed conversations he had had with his legal representative. Having a great deal of available time in the confines of his detention center accommodations, Calvin poured over every facet and detail in his case, preparing for his next legal juncture. As his efforts seemed futile, he searched one last time for a viable defense. *It's impossible* he concluded as he slouched in his chair, dropping his head. The memory of the last visitation his attorney paid him at the jail confirmed that notion. He recalled the conversation vividly.

Separated by the broad bulletproof glass, he and his attorney picked up the receiver mounted on the cool concrete wall and discussed the probability of winning before a jury.

"Calvin! I just don't see it happening." his attorney said, shaking his head.

"You aren't even trying!" Calvin exclaimed in frustration.

"Calvin. A jury convicted Dave three weeks ago and the judge put him away for twenty years with no parole, and he didn't do the shooting. What do you think a jury will do to you once the State's Attorney shows them a picture of the hole you blew in that boy's chest with that shotgun? I mean really, what the hell were you thinking?" he asked.

"I don't know," Calvin sighed.

"Calvin, I think the offer the State has put on the table is a good one. Forty-five years with no parole for first degree murder isn't a bad deal you know? They could have sought the death penalty."

"It's bullshit, if you ask me!"

"But you killed a man; I mean really. You got pissed off, went and stole a shotgun, and then drove across the county and blew this guy away. The state could easily argue premeditation, a jury would find you guilty, and a judge could sentence you to life—might as well be a death sentence 'cause you'd die in jail"

Calvin hung his head and quickly did the math "But I'll be 68 years old when I'm eligible for release."

"…and hopefully you'll be too old to kill anyone else." his attorney added.

Now as he sat quietly in the slate blue swivel chair, Calvin Miller took in the courtroom's atmosphere. With his parents seated in the galley, showing their support, Calvin turned around and gave them a small nod as a short greeting before returning his focus to the judge who emerged from the back door and was ascending the bench.

"All rise for the Honorable Thomas Henderson, Sr.," the

bailiff cried out.

Taking a seat in his chair, the judge pulled himself up to his desk, poured a cup of iced cold water from the chilled carafe, and greeted the two attorneys standing poised behind their respective tables.

"Your Honor, the State would like to call the matter of the State versus Calvin Miller before the court this morning," Beth Collins announced while opening her summary folder.

"Very well." The judge shifted in his seat, preparing for a lengthy legal argument. "Counsel, your client is charged with murder in the second degree. How does your client intend to plea today?"

"Well, your Honor, I wanted to make a preliminary request for a postponement," the attorney announced, shocking both the State's Attorney and the judge. The parties, having already had preliminary discussions about the case, anticipated Calvin Miller pleading guilty, taking the State's gracious offer.

"Counsel!" the judge yelled, infuriated at the notion to even suggest a postponement, "this case has already been postponed a number of times." Yanking the folder from the side of the bench, the judge violently flipped through the pages. "A postponement was granted to the defense back in October because, as you indicated, Mr. Anderson, you needed more time to interview your witnesses. Then again in December, the State requested a postponement because certain DNA examinations were completed but still needed to be verified, and we didn't want to get into an appeals situation, which brought us to March when I granted you another postponement because you indicated the court appointed psychiatrist hadn't finished her report from her examination of Mr. Miller. Now you have the audacity to ask me for another postponement, Mr. Anderson? What, pray tell, do you need another postponement for, Mr. Anderson?"

Anderson drew in a deep breath humbly submitting his excuse to the court. "Your Honor, we just received the psychiatrist's report, and I would like the opportunity to subpoena expert witnesses on behalf of my client—"

"Mr. Anderson! According to my file, your client was

examined in April and the psychiatrist's report was filed by the end of that same month. It's now July and this case is almost a year old."

"But your Honor, I—"

"But nothing!" the judge retorted as he slammed the folder down off to the side of the desk. "You've had ample time to prepare for the case; your request for a postponement is denied."

Disappointed with the loss of his last legal maneuver, the defense counsel submitted to the court, "Your Honor, it is Mr. Miller's intentions to enter a guilty plea."

With the anticipated proceedings now back on course, Beth Collins extracted the statement of charges from her summary folder and, in narrative form, recounted the events as Jones and Lang had documented them in their reports. Reading into the record the official account of the murder of Austin Michaels, the audience in the galley, most assembling for unrelated matters before the court, sat silently with an attentive ear as the horrific details of the murder were revealed. A lone reporter from the Baltimore Sun sat in the third row, scribbling down the details for the crime report column, racing against an early afternoon deadline.

Calvin sat stoic as his actions were recounted, causing many to wince at the thought of dying in such a manner. His effect unmoved, the stone-faced defendant awaited the inevitable. *Might as well get it over with and start doing my time.* His thoughts drifted away from the audible rendition of the murder. *The sooner I get in and start pulling my time, the sooner I get out.*

Having finished her recitation of the events, Judge Henderson looked over at the defense table and waited for Mr. Anderson and his client to stand and receive the official verdict.

"Mr. Miller," said the judge as the defense attorney motioned for Calvin to stand up. "I find that there are sufficient facts to support your guilty plea and do hereby find you guilty of murder in the second degree. Now, as for sentencing—"

"Your Honor, I was under the impression you would be issuing a presentence investigation before rendering a sentence today," interjected Mr. Anderson.

"No, sir, not today," the judge answered. "Today's proceeding, Counsel, was one in which you and your client were pleading guilty to an agreed sentence term, is it not?"

"Yes, your Honor, but I was—"

"Therefore, I am not issuing a PSI. At your request, Counsel, I've already bound myself to this agreement." Turning his attention to Calvin, the judge then issued the sentence. "Mr. Miller, having found you guilty of second degree murder, I hereby sentence you to incarceration at the Maryland Department of Corrections for forty-five years, without the possibility of parole."

"Your Honor, are you suspending any of that time or offering counseling for my client?" Mr. Anderson quickly asked.

"No Counsel, I am not. Your client killed a citizen of this county. If he wants any counseling he can talk to his cellmates. God knows he'll have plenty of time for that."

****

With his head resting in the palm of his hand, Charles slowly pushed the cursor around the computer screen, proofreading the message once again before clicking the submit button. *There, it's done.* Though the message was instantaneous, Nicholae, whose undivided attention was focused on his own report concerning the Brady account, didn't notice the new email message momentarily flash across the screen before disappearing. Line by line, Nicholae went through the account folder and jotted down his notes onto an empty pad that was quickly filling with questions to be posed to the derelict manager.

I don't understand why this account hasn't been settled yet? Tossing the tablet onto his desktop, Nicholae was perturbed at the obvious indolence. Having nearly filled the front page of his tablet with his raised issues, Nicholae grabbed the account folder and tablet, and stomped off to confront Charles.

Charles was sitting behind his desk, his head still cradled in hand, as he dragged the two of hearts onto the third stack in his quiet little game of solitaire. Charles jerked upright when his office door burst open.

"No wonder this account isn't closed!" Nicholae said. "It interferes with your solitaire games, does it not?" he asked in his rich Russian dialect.

"Did you get my email?" Charles asked out of sync.

"Huh?" replied Nicholae.

"Did you get my email?" Charles asked again. "There's something I need to talk to you about."

"What email?"

"I sent you an email asking to meet with you in my office today at 1:00 after lunch. But seeing that you're here, we can talk now." Charles offered as he gestured for Nicholae to take a seat in the empty chair in front of his desk.

Nicholae accepted the invitation. He needed answers and was certain that this meeting would reveal more about what was keeping Charles from pushing his loan officers along and getting more work done. Business was booming, and there was no time for games.

Nicholae pulled the chair out from behind the computer monitor and faced it directly towards Charles, taking his seat. Charles stood up and slowly made his way over to the office door, pushing it shut for more privacy. Resting the account folder on his crossed legs, Nicholae said nothing as he patiently waited for Charles to initiate the meeting.

"Mr. Kozlov, for the past eight months my group and I have been working very hard for the Walcott Financial Group," he said, circling back around his desk and returning to his seat. "But, there has been no show of appreciation for the work we've done so far! Everyday, my employees and I come in here, bright and early, working on these accounts, and we stay late into the night, often past midnight, to make sure that everything gets done. But bosses like you don't appreciate us, do you?"

"Charles, I—" Nicholae said.

"Excuse me," Charles said as he reached into the top right desk drawer, pulled out his .44 magnum revolver, and leveled it at his boss, "but I think I was talking."

Nicholae's eyes widened, alarmed at the sudden presence of the pistol. Sliding the folder onto the front of Charles' desk, Nicholae went to stand up.

"I think that—" Nicholae uttered before being interrupted.

"I think that you'd better set your ass back down," Charles demanded of his boss.

Nicholae froze midstream, raising his hands in the air to show he was offering no resistance.

"Charles, put the gun down, nobody needs to get hurt," Nicholae said in a soothing voice.

"No, no, I don't think so! You just need to stay seated and finish listening to me," Charles said with a menacing glare.

"Now what was I saying? Ah yes… my employees working hard. It seems to me, Mr. Kozlov, that you have a lack of appreciation for me and my staff. We're well ahead of last year's pace and still it isn't enough for you or the big bosses, is it? No, you're sitting over in your office yelling and screaming at everyone so that at the end of the year you can get that big fat bonus check. But really, don't you think that we peons deserve that bonus? After all, we're the grunts who made the money, aren't we?"

"Look, Charles, if it's about the money—"

"It's not about the money. It's about the respect. Don't you get it?"

"Charles, look, put the gun down and we'll talk about setting better hours, I can—"

"You don't get it do you?" Charles said as he squared the iron sights straight at Nicholae's forehead.

"Get what, Charles?" Nicholae said as fear soared through every ounce of his body.

"I don't care anymore," Charles said with a little wave of the pistol and half-crazed smile.

The sudden explosion from the .44 magnum caliber bullet exploding through Nicolae's head startled everyone seated in their cubicle just outside Charles' office door. As a gray pink mist sprayed against the back wall and splattered against the frosted office door window, Nicholae met death instantaneously. Charles stood up and looked over his desk, waiting for the smoke to clear to see if his target would require a second, more lethal shot. Waving the smoke away, he continued to train the end of his pistol towards his dead target.

Charles never heard the door open for the ringing in his ears. Without notice, Martha stood in the doorway, aghast at the scene unfolding before her eyes.

"Get out of here, Martha!" Charles shouted as he waved the gun. "You don't want to be in here."

With a shocked look, Martha grabbed the doorknob and slung the door shut as she turned and ran back towards her cubicle. Reaching into her purse, she grabbed her cell phone. Martha frantically dialed the numbers. Other employees stood at their workstations, disoriented and dismayed. *We've got to get out of here,* one employee thought, making his way towards the exit. As the remaining employees followed in suit, they were stunned to an abrupt halt when the second shot rang out. The muffled sharp explosion, accompanied by a brilliant white flash, resonated as shards of glass fell to the floor.

Unable to catch her breath, Martha's fear overwhelmed her as she realized her feet weren't keeping up with her will. She desperately tried to flee as fast as possible, but her feet wouldn't move fast enough, causing her to stumble down the first half of the flight of steps. Stopping on the landing for a few seconds, Martha was able to dial 911 and depress the send button as she finished descending the second half of the steps, sprinting out into the parking lot and across the street.

"911, what is your emergency?"

"There's been a—a—a shooting. Please hurry. Get the police here."

"Ma'am where are you?"

Martha, winded from her flight, drew in several deep breaths before she was able to convey the location of her office building and where on the second floor she had last seen the shooter.

"Dispatch to all available units, we have a report of an

active shooter on the second floor of the Walcott Financial Group Building off Madison and Chesapeake Drive. I need all available units to respond. Medics are currently being notified and will be staging nearby until units can advise when the scene is safe."

The radio airway sprang to life as multiple units keyed up to relay they were enroute to the shooting spree. Marked patrol units, with emergency lights blazing and sirens screaming recklessly sped through the congested business district, arriving quickly at the scene in an effort to contain the situation and at least save someone's life.

"7-Edward-10 dispatch, do I have any units out there with a patrol rifle?" asked the patrol sergeant.

Looking over his shoulder to verify that his M16 was strapped in the safety mount on the patrol car's cage, the officer grabbed his lapel mic and clicked the transmission button.

"7-Adam-27 dispatch, I have my patrol rifle," acknowledged the patrol officer.

"7-Edward-10 dispatch, advise 7-Adam-27 to deploy his rifle, assemble a team, and neutralize the threat," the radio squawked, followed by a second of silence as those tuned into the channel taking in the severity of the call for service.

"7-Edward-27, I'm direct."

****

Officer Martin pulled his patrol unit up next to the neighboring office building and removed the M16 from its mount. Sliding back the action and letting it slam home free, Martin readied his weapon as he looked up and picked three fellow officers to enter the building with him.

"What do we know?" Martin asked.

"According to witnesses, the shooter is a white male, 55 to 65 years in age, has white hair, beard and mustache, glasses, and was wearing a dark-blue polo shirt and tan khaki pants with loafers. He's supposed to be up in this corner of the building and armed with a handgun," one officer rattled off.

"You guys ready?" Martin asked.

The four officers double-timed to the corner stairwell, extracting their side arms from their holsters as Martin took the point position with the M16. As one officer pulled open the exterior door to the stairwell, Martin aimed the M16 directly towards the shadowed area, hoping his eyes would quickly adjust from the bright sunlight to the darkened cavity beneath the stairs. Martin whisked into the bottom landing, giving a quick peek around the dark corner under the stairs to be sure it was clear.

"Is it clear?" one officer asked.

"I can't see," Martin answered.

Without request, a flashlight illuminated the area beneath the stairs, revealing nothing in the dark shadows.

"Clear," Martin whispered retraining his attention on the flight of steps the team needed to climb.

Focusing the attention of the rifle's sights towards the second floor landing, the officers took up a four-man formation and meticulously walked up the steps, taking each step as quietly as possible to avoid alerting the shooter of their presence. When they reached the landing of the second floor the two rear officers aimed their dull finished Sig Sauer SP2340 handguns in opposing directions; one towards the third floor and one back towards the first floor, eliminating any surprise attack.

"We breach the door on three," said Martin. "One, two, three—"

As they flung the metal door open, Martin nosed around the sturdy door jam, the muzzle of the assault rifle leading the way. He could smell the gun smoke lingering in the hallway before him.

"Cubicles on the left, offices on the right; let's clear the cubicles first," Martin said.

The stick of four officers inched their way up towards the opening in the cubicle. With Martin focusing on any attack that may commence from the cubicle area, the next two officers trained their sight picture on the two office doors as the last officer concentrated on guarding the rear.

Martin rounded the corner into the cubicle, finding three open stations that made quick work for clearing the area. Giving a thumbs-up and acknowledging that the area was clear; Martin pointed towards the closed office doors as their next point of concern.

Stacking up on each side of the first door, Martin kicked the door open and the four officers converged into the small office. *Empty. Where the hell is he?* Martin turned and noticed the broken picture and shattered glass lying on the floor from the wall separating the two offices. Exiting the first office, Martin assembled his team around the second office door. This time, he decided, he would try the door handle first.

Twisting the doorknob very gingerly, he felt it break free from the latch, and pushed open the door. In an instant, the four officers scurried into the office.

"Oh, shit!" the third officer yelled as he lost his footing and nearly fell into the pool of blood.

Martin made his way in as far as was possible, focusing his sights on the head of the subject lying on the floor behind the desk.

"He's dead already," Martin said.

"This one is, too," another officer indicated.

Martin turned and saw the lifeless body of the second subject, sprawled across the floor, and wondered how he even missed seeing the dead man when making the entry.

Turning his gaze back onto the subject lying behind the desk, Martin recalled the description of the suspected shooter and noted the nickel-plated .44 magnum laying beside his disfigured head. A star-shaped bullet wound with significant stippling oozed blood saturating the dark gray carpet.

"Look's like we found our shooter."

136

CHAPTER THIRTEEN

As the morning sun chased away the bitter cold that enveloped the row home community, Doris kissed her husband goodbye and descended into the unfinished basement where she set up her ancient computer system and plunged in to surf the Internet. Pointing her mouse to certain desired destinations, Doris followed link after link to exotic islands and cruise lines as she completed price comparisons to find the most extravagant getaway deal available.

Her informational pursuit was relentless. Sipping her morning black coffee, she carefully reviewed each of her search engine results. *Carnival, Royal Caribbean, and oh, Norwegian. Better stick with Carnival, they're the cheapest.*

With a passing click, Doris navigated her way to Carnival's Sensation, sporting three cruises scheduled for the Bahamas this coming January. The Sensation's Club Vegas Casino caught her eye. Doris daydreamed about her and Fred playing Texas Hold'em together late into the night while drifting out at sea. Lost in the moment, Doris suddenly became annoyed at the eruption of the Disney Channel on the upstairs television that was now drowning out her dreams.

"Stevie! Turn that shit down!" she yelled to her four-year-old son.

Looking back to the computer monitor, and trying to

refocus her thoughts, Doris navigated to her Favorites button and slapped the mouse button. Scrolling down the menu, she found the VacationsToGo.com link and entered the site to find the latest deals. She found the $539 per person price on the Carnival still just a little too steep for her budget. As the living room television continued to blare, Doris again became annoyed. Letting loose an exasperating sigh, she shuffled her way to the foot of the stairs as she sucked in a deep hard breath.

"Stevie! I said turn that shit down, damn it!"

Doris went back over to her dark damp corner where the water pipes continued with their usual clanking noise; undoubtedly, the toilet had been running all night again.

"Damn it, Fred!" she cussed, knowing he wasn't even home. "When are you going to fix that piece of shit?"

Doris let out a low groan, trying to ignore the blaring television and the banging pipes.

Why does everybody keep pissing me off? Focusing on the picturesque seaside and thatched hut resting in the shade of the swaying palm trees, Doris' imagination carried her and Fred off to such a place, where the peaceful waves rolled over her feet as she sipped on her favorite umbrella concoction escaping the drudgery of the dilapidated blue-collared neighborhood.

****

Next to Christmas, Saint Patrick's Day was one of the most celebrated days in the police department, particularly among the CID detectives with Irish blood running through their veins. For those who lacked seniority and didn't have the Luck of the Irish, getting the day off proved challenging. So, on this day, Detective Lang and acting Sergeant Winthrop were the only two homicide detectives staffed to handle any death investigations that may arise on this notorious day.

"Look," Winthrop said in his rich Baltimore accent, "if anything comes out we're on our own!"

Attending to a supplemental report that needed proofread and edited, Lang pursued the numerous employee interviews from the Walcott Financial Office murder-suicide case. Lang flipped open his notebook and then re-read each of the written statements from the witnesses he had interviewed. Most of them acknowledged they had not seen, or knew anything about the events leading up to the shooting. A majority confided they had heard two distinct gunshots sometime just before lunch. Regardless, the medical examiner's office already conducted the autopsies. From the threatening email from Charles, coupled with the suicide note left behind at his residence prior to setting out for work, it was quite apparent that Charles Hancock had every intention of killing Mr. Kozlov before taking his own life. The only things that remained unfinished in the investigation were the supplemental reports required to document the events of the investigation.

As Lang inserted the generic information into the header and footer of the supplemental report, Melanie, the unit's office assistant, entered the squad room.

"Keith! I just got a call from the shift commander at the Fourteenth District. They've got a dead four year old, says something doesn't look right."

"Did they say how they think he died?" Winthrop asked.

"No, just that he was found unconscious and was transported to the ER where they pronounced him dead." she replied.

Winthrop mused. *So much for going out and getting hammered tonight.*

There were no two ways about it. One detective would have to respond to the hospital and deal with the family while the second would go to the house and conduct the legal obligations of searching the house for any explanation for the sudden and unexplained death. Winthrop set out to meet the family in the emergency room, Lang grabbed the laptop computer, anticipating the necessity of a search warrant for the residence that district personnel were currently securing.

****

Pulling onto Church Lane, Lang noticed the group of

139

uniformed officers huddled together in a front yard, clearly marking the exact residence.

"Hey, Kenny," one officer said.

"What's the story here?" Lang asked.

"911 got a call for an unconscious subject. Medics got here, Mom says she found her four-year old unresponsive on the living room couch. Medics didn't have a pulse or respiration and transported the kid to the ER; sounds like he got a courtesy ride."

"Anything in the house that should concern us?" Lang inquired.

"We only got in as far as the living room. You can see where the kid was lying on the couch, eating popcorn, and watching cartoons," another officer offered.

"Well a judge isn't going to sign a search warrant based on that, and waiting for the pathology report to come back isn't going to cut it," Lang said.

"How long does that take?" the officer asked.

"Ten weeks, easily," Lang said.

"Hell, that gives the family plenty of time to get rid of any evidence; providing this turns out to be a murder."

"No way," another officer chimed in. "When I talked to Mom, she said t her son was sick; this is probably a medical death," the officer said.

"I don't know, Mom didn't look too concerned when they were carting the kid off in the ambo. If it were my son, I would have been freaking out," another said.

"All right, let's keep the house secured, and I'll only need one of you for that. I'll start knocking out some interviews with the neighbors and see if we can shed some light on what was going on today," Lang said.

Lang surveyed the street and quickly determined that based on the number of curious neighbors standing on their front porch taking in the action, most, if not all, would have some information to contribute to the investigation regardless of it relevance. Noticing an older woman standing in her entryway next door, holding her steaming cup of Joe and hair still tightly spun on foamy curlers, Lang gave a half-hearted smile and started towards the door. Seeing that the detective was heading her way, she quickly vanished into the depths of her abode. Following a firm knock that rattled the metal screen door, the lady returned, now garbed in a tattered pink house coat, sipping from her coffee mug.

"Can I help you?" she asked after gulping her slurp, her southern drawl evident.

"I sure hope so, ma'am. I'm Detective Lang with the Criminal Investigation Division. May I come in and speak with you about your neighbors?"

Being privy to most community gossip, the resident couldn't resist the request.

"Absolutely, Officer. Come on in. Please, have a seat right here," she said, moving the morning newspaper off one end of the couch. "What's going on?" she asked, needing to satisfy her urge to know.

"Well, I'm sorry to say that the little boy next door, Stevie, died this morning," Lang said remorsefully.

"Oh, no! That's so sad," she said, shaking her head before taking another sip.

"I wanted to stop by to see if you had seen or heard anything suspicious this morning from next door," Lang prodded.

"There's always something going on next door," she explained with a glaring look of disapproval. "Like a few weeks ago when we had that unexpected snow. Stevie went out and was playing in it for at least an hour without any coat on before his mother realized it! She's always on that Internet; she never watches him. He got real sick from being out in the cold without a coat, you know? I don't think she ever took him to the doctor."

Lang jotted down a few notes then looked back up at the placid wrinkled face hovering over the brim of her mug. "So, what about today? Did you see or hear anything?" Lang asked.

"Oh, yeah, you did ask that. Yeah, I heard some stuff— typical shit from next door. She's always screaming and yelling at him/ It started this morning, I guess it was around 8:30, he turned on the TV and she started yelling at him from the basement to turn it off," she said.

"Is that all you heard?" Lang asked.

"No, it's not. She yelled at him several times throughout the morning. Then I heard a strange sound. You know, their stairs are right against my living room wall and I kept hearing this noise like someone was walking up the steps followed by this thumping noise going back down the stairs."

"And?"

"And that happened about two or three times then it got real quiet over there...at least until you all showed up," she said.

Lang thanked the lady for the information and excused himself back out to the sidewalk where he met up with one of the officers.

"Did she have anything to say?" he asked.

"Oh, yeah, looks like we have enough to get a search warrant now."

****

Assembling the application for the legal document came effortlessly as Lang accessed the laptop, punched in the address and house description, followed by a brief synopsis of the unexpected death investigation. Lang intentionally documented the description of the mother's unexpressive demeanor and the neighbor's account of the repeated thumping noises, hoping to leave a lasting impression with the judge who would be reviewing the application. Having printed out the document on the portable printer, Lang drove less than two miles from the residence to the local district courthouse where most of the judges had finished their morning docket and were preparing for their lunch break. Lang raced by the bailiff's posted at the front door with his credentials held high into the air. Dawdling for even a minute could inevitably result in missing the judges who wouldn't want their lunch disturbed and waiting for the next two hours would certainly keep the two detectives well into the night processing the scene.

"What do you have, Ken?" one bailiff called out.

142

"I need a judge ASAP. I have an application for a search warrant I need reviewed."

"Come with me."

The bailiff turned the corner to the side door that was armed with a five-button cipher lock that he accessed in seconds. Swinging the door open, the bailiff scurried through the records department and bustled through the rear corridor, poking his head into one judge's chamber after another. Coming up empty, the bailiff froze as he stuck his head into the fourth door and found one judge who had lingered just a little too long.

"Judge, Detective Lang from the Homicide Unit is here. He has an application for a search warrant he needs reviewed. Do you mind?"

Lang could hear the familiar voice from his patrol days as Judge Susan Thompson instructed the bailiff to see him into her chambers. Lang rounded the corner and greeted his former legal acquaintance.

"Judge Thompson! How have you been?" Lang said offering a handshake.

"Detective Lang, I haven't seen you in years! So, you're in the Homicide Unit, now?"

"For about a year and a half. I see that you haven't moved too far from the old district courthouse."

"Nope. I've been here five years now. Can you believe it?" she asked wondering how time had escaped her. "So, what do you have for me, today?" she asked holding out her hand.

"Well, your Honor, we have an unattended death of a four-year-old here in this district. There are a couple of unusual things about it--not that any death is straightforward, but we'd like to get into the house and have a look-see to make sure everything is on the up and up," Lang explained.

"All right, let me have a look."

****

Decorated with a plush couch, matching chair, and freshly-cut flowers situated in a vase on the coffee table, the family room afforded Winthrop as private of a location as could be expected for the circumstances. Mrs. Riley, joined by her husband, Frederick, were seated next to each other; her husband comforting her the best he knew how while she dabbed away her tears.

"I don't know what I'm going to do without him," she whimpered.

"God will see us through this, you'll see, Doris," said her husband.

"Mr. and Mrs. Riley, I really need to get through this interview. Would it be possible to speak with each of you alone, apart from one another? It's important that we maintain the integrity of the investigation and can show that no one party compromised the other's account of the events. This really shouldn't take too long," Winthrop explained.

"Sure. Absolutely, Detective," said Frederick. "Who do you want to speak to first?"

"Well, sir, I'd think that maybe you and I should talk first and give your wife a few moments to compose herself," Winthrop suggested.

Almost as if orchestrated, a nurse entered the room and escorted Doris into another family room that happened to be unoccupied at the time. Leaving Mr. Riley and the detective alone, Winthrop got right to business.

Winthrop pulled his steno pad from his jacket pocket and gave a solid click on the end of his pen. "Mr. Riley, can you tell me about what happened this morning?"

"Stevie's been sick, so we've been letting him sleep as much as possible. I got up like I do every other weekday, got ready for work down at the port, and headed into work at 6:00 a.m.," Frederick paused, fighting to find some level of composure that would enable him to finish giving his account. Drawing in a deep breath, he continued, "Sometime after nine, Doris called me and said that something was wrong with Stevie," he said, unable to hold back the tears streaming down his cheeks, "and that the ambulance was on the way to the house. By the time I got home," Frederick paused again, looking away from the detective "the ambulance was there, and

Stevie was dead!"

"They didn't pronounce him dead until he arrived at the hospital. What made you think he was dead?" Winthrop asked.

"When I pulled up in front of the house, the paramedic was carrying his limp little body down the front sidewalk. When I glanced into his eyes, there was nothing there. That's when I knew," he said sorrowfully.

****

The white suburban van appropriately marked "Crime Lab" pulled up in front of the residence with Lang following closely behind.

"You got it signed?" the uniformed officer asked.

"Yep. Time to get to work."

Forensic Technician Lauren James pulled the side panel door open, climbed up into the side of the van, and started piling black cases of equipment at the door's edge.

"Okay, guys. I could use a hand carrying all of this into the house," she said.

Grabbing every piece of equipment, the three entered the residence, firmly closing the front storm door in their wake.

"I'll have to get photographs first before you guys start tearing into everything," Lauren said.

"It's a search warrant, but we don't know what were looking for, so there won't be much tearing until we get a lot of looking done first," Lang explained.

"Suit yourself," Lauren replied, "but either way, I've got to get the photos done first!"

"It's all yours," Lang said surrendering the scene to the forensic technician.

Popping open the heavy-duty metal hasps on the scarred case, Lauren reached in, lugged out the 35mm digital beast, and slung the weighty device around her neck. Installing a fresh pack of batteries and empty media card, Lauren prepared for the long haul, imagining the homicide detective would be requesting photographs of every possible aspect of the residence as usually was the case. Depressing the power switch, the high-pitched tone working in concert with the flickering lights announced the equipment had sprung to life and was prepared for action.

"Where do you want to begin?" Lauren asked, having no information about the case.

"We'll, we're already in the living room where Mom found the boy," Lang said.

"A boy? A boy is our victim? How old is he?" Lauren asked suddenly, taken back.

"He was four," Lang said.

"My son is only three! How the hell does a four-year-old boy die on a couch watching cartoons?" she asked, seeing the television still broadcasting the Cartoon Network.

"That's what we're here to find out," Lang answered.

****

"Mr. Riley, I have just a few more questions for you before I take a moment to speak with your wife," Winthrop explained.

"Sure, Detective, what is it?"

"Can you explain to me your relationship with Doris? I mean, I know you're married, but you're forty-seven years old and she's only twenty-four. How did the two of you hook up?" Winthrop said inquisitively.

Frederick laughed at the question. It was one that he had become used to and enjoyed telling the story. One person came off a rocky relationship while the other had just finished settling a divorce. Frederick recounted how he and Doris met, fell in love, and started raising a family.

"She had just come out of a bad relationship. Her ex-boyfriend liked to use her as his punching bag. He never could control the whiskey. I knew her through a friend of the family and would often bump into her and her jackass boyfriend down at the tavern. You see, I love country music, and they have live country western bands there every Friday and Saturday night. Problem was, my wife didn't like me drinking the paycheck away every Friday night, so I came home to find she had packed all of her shit and left," Frederick said, shaking with a slight grin growing on his face. "Good thing she did or I would have never met Doris."

Winthrop sat back in his chair, amused at the direction that the conversation had taken. He had been in a similar situation himself, once married, now divorced and remarried—he knew this story all too well.

"With her ex gone and my wife leaving me, we started talking at the bar, commiserating over our Coors Light about how screwed up we let our lives get. Pretty soon, we realized we had a lot in common. She wanted a good man who worked hard; I wanted a woman who wasn't always on my ass about drinking beer. Next thing you know, we were running off to the courthouse getting hitched," he said with a wide grin.

Frederick gave every indication his memories were fond ones. Then, rather haphazardly, he turned the direction of his conversation to the current wrangling down at the marine terminal. How he had been skipped over for a promotion he could never understand.

"Twenty-seven years I've been there! And what do I have to show for it? Nothing, just an old piece-of-shit row home, a broken-hearted wife, and two dead sons!"

"*Two* dead sons?" Winthrop asked, sitting straight up in his chair.

"Why yes, detective; didn't you know that Stevie had a younger brother, Timothy, who died about two years ago?"

"No, no I didn't."

CHAPTER FOURTEEN

The intense beam from the compact flashlight streaked through the darkened stairwell that led to the musty, unfinished basement. As Lang followed Lauren down the wooden creaky steps, they gave careful attention to each step to insure they did not disturb anything that would indicate what happened to Stevie earlier that morning.

"Why don't people put lights in these basements?" Lauren asked, already becoming irritated at the poor living conditions.

"I don't know. Do you see anything on the edge of the steps that might appear to be fresh?" Lang asked, refocusing the conversation back to the case at hand.

"No. Why?" Lauren asked.

"The neighbor next door said she heard someone repeatedly walking up the steps and a thumping noise heading down the steps," Lang explained.

"Probably the laundry basket," Lauren offered.

"Could be, we'll have to look for the—hey, wait! What's that?" Lang asked pointing to the bottom of the steps.

"What's what?" Lauren asked, searching with the beam of her light for whatever it was that caught Lang's eye.

"That," Lang said, pointing again as the light streamed over the irregular dark stain on the gray concrete floor.

The two investigators carefully finished descending the

148

wooden staircase, stooping over their new find.

"Holy shit! It looks like a puddle of dried blood," Lauren exclaimed. "We can swab it up and do a presumptive test on it right here if you'd like, Ken," she offered.

"Absolutely! But let's make sure we go over this staircase one more time. If this is blood, it's got to be somewhere else, too," Lang said.

Lauren carefully walked back up the stairs inspecting each step before firmly planting her foot. Reaching the top of the stairs, she opened another hard case container and extracted a bottle of saline water, Q-tip swabs, test packet, and the evidence envelopes that would secure the samples.

Returning to the bottom of the basement steps, she saturated a Q-tip and rubbed it on one edge of the stain on the floor.

"This is really dry," she said, "it wouldn't be this dry if it's blood from today!"

Lifting the Q-tip to just inches from her eyes, Lauren confirmed that the dark, dry particles had entangled themselves in the spun cotton on the tip's end.

"Hold this," she said, handing her flashlight off to Lang.

With great care and proficiency, Lauren held the Q-tip sample with one hand as she opened the test kit with the other, a feat that she had undoubtedly performed a hundred times before. Holding the bottle with the eye-dropper tip hovered over the swab, she gently pinched the bottle with just enough pressure to allow one drop of solution to fall onto the swab's tip.

"It's blood," she announced as the chemical compounds instantly reacted and turned brilliant pink in color.

"Yeah, but whose? And when did it get here?" Lang pondered aloud.

****

A woolen blanket draped around her shoulders, Doris came out from the back room and found a place on the couch in front of Detective Winthrop.

"Doris, honey, I'll be right here in the back if you need me; I'm not going far." Frederick said as a uniformed officer escorted him away from his wife and the detective.

"Mrs. Riley, how are you doing now?" Winthrop asked.

"Better," she said with a flat affect.

"I've had a chance to talk to your husband. Other than what the first uniformed officer has explained to me from your brief conversation with him, I can't say that I really know much about what happened this morning at the house and was hoping you could help me out with that." Winthrop paused, offering a simple frown.

"I don't know what happened! I was down stairs on the Internet looking up some travel information on cruise lines and went upstairs and found Stevie lying on the couch," she paused, letting the scene replay in her mind. Her eyes welling up, she continued, "He wasn't breathing, so I called 911 to get some help!"

****

Every inch of the basement had been searched; and short of the one official blood stain, the only other item that seemed to have any evidentiary value was the computer in the corner whose colorful twisting pipes screensaver emitted an iridescent glow against the concrete block wall.

"We're taking the computer," Lang directed.

"Okay," Lauren replied, "Do you know how big of a pain in the butt that is, especially on a sudden death case?".

"Yep, I sure do, and we're still taking it," Lang said with a grimace. Lauren wiggled the mouse, forcing the colorful animated pipes to fade away, revealing the Carnival Cruise Line website with scantly clad women circled around a thatch-hut bar, exotic drinks propped in their hand.

"Can you explain something to me?" Lauren demanded.

"What's that?"

"How does a chick with no job, living in a dump like this, with a husband who makes half the money I make, afford a cruise? I must be doing something wrong," she said.

Snapping a picture of the computer screen, Lang pulled the plug on the computer and bagged up the CPU into a brown paper bag. Feeling confident they had completely finished processing the basement, Lang and Lauren collected their finds and carried them upstairs; setting them on the living room floor next to the front door where the uniformed officer stood posted.

"How long is this going to take?" the officer asked while glancing at his watch.

"We're going to hit the first floor now, then the upstairs—we're definitely going to be here for a while. Why? You got a hot date tonight?"

"Nope. Doesn't matter to me; it all pays the same. Sarge was just checking in on me."

"Well, call him back on the radio and tell him you're doing just fine," Lang cracked.

Milling around the living room, Lang took the opportunity to look around behind and beneath the furniture, tipping each one over to ensure a thorough look.

"Lauren, when you were going through the house and taking your initial photographs, did you notice all these bowls lying around?" Lang asked.

"Yeah. Some are empty, but most have popcorn and something melted in it. Any ideas?" she asked.

Walking into the narrow kitchen, Lang immediately spied the empty box of Orville Redenbacher popcorn lying on the kitchen counter, just beneath the microwave shelf where a paint-spattered stepstool stood in the middle of the floor.

"I bet you the melted sticky stuff is ice cream," Lang said as he popped open the freezer door revealing the three ice cream quarts whose lids were not firmly in place with lumps of frozen ice cream caked on their sides.

"Popcorn mixed with ice cream? What gives?" Lauren asked.

"A hungry kid," answered Lang.

Beginning to see the signs of child neglect, Lauren re-secured her 35mm camera and painstakingly found every abandoned bowl laden with stale popcorn and melted ice cream. There were fourteen in all when the investigators finished their search. And there were three bedrooms and a bathroom on the second floor that still needed to be processed.

"Ready to do the bedroom?" Lauren asked Lang, offering a wink in jest.

"It's gotta get done sometime," Lang said, smiling as he followed her up the stairs.

"You know, when I was taking pictures in the master bedroom, I saw a screwdriver lying on the floor next to the television. There was a worn-out spot on the floor. You might want to give it a look see also," Lauren suggested as she organized her equipment in the upstairs hallway.

Lang turned the corner and entered the cramped master bedroom. It was an absolute miracle to see how anyone could fit a king-sized bed, dresser, bureau, and television stand into the ten foot by ten foot room. Somehow, the Riley family had managed such a feat.

One couldn't help but walk upon the piles of clothes strewn about most of the battered hardwood floor surrounding the bed. A one-foot wide path around the bed gave little for a walkway. The dresser and bureau were both littered with discarded plates bearing rotting and moldy food.

Lang surveyed the overall condition of the living space and tried to imagine how anyone could rest comfortably with so much junk and clutter littering the room. As Lang looked into the corner of the room, a small television unit setting atop a small round table grabbed his attention. *That's funny! Why in the world would you...*

Noticing the television screen pointed away from the bed, his glance fell to the orange and black screwdriver lying on the floor where Lauren had recalled it laying. The Stanley screwdriver wasn't haphazardly lying on the floor. Couldn't have been. It was precisely placed flush against the dark stained baseboard immediately next to the closet door. *But why?* Lang considered the oddity of the room's layout as he knelt down closer to the floor to examine the placement of the screwdriver. *Why would you...?* That's when he noticed the gouges in the hardwood flooring. Seeing the curved pattern that matched the direction of the door's swing, Lang was perplexed at the scene.

Standing up, Lang stepped back and continued to survey what he was seeing.

I've never seen this before, he mused to himself.

Stepping up to peer into the tiny closet space, the horrific revelation suddenly overwhelmed him. *Oh, God! No, it can't be!* He tried to reason another explanation for what he was seeing, but no other logical explanation came to mind. Retreating in order to take in the whole scene, Lang was certain. Certain of his conclusion, Lang whipped out his cell phone and dialed.

****

Winthrop was growing weary of the circles Doris Riley had steered him in during the past hour. Having talked about everything from her early childhood in Baltimore, the schools she attended, her failed attempt at community college, and finally to her meeting and marrying Frederick, Doris talked Detective Winthrop's ear off and he had nothing to show for it. Giddy, like a young schoolgirl, Doris expressed how much she had enjoyed getting to know Detective Winthrop.

"Can I call you Keith?" she asked, learning his first name as she looked at his business card.

"Detective Winthrop is fine," he replied, smiling back at her giddiness.

His cell phone vibrated, surprising Winthrop. It seemed strange he was receiving service deep within the confines of the hospital; usually the steel beams and thick walls prevented a connection. Grabbing his phone, Winthrop saw Lang's name and number on the caller ID screen and flipped the phone open. He decided he needed a respite from Doris and answered the call as he walked into a distant corner in search of some privacy

"What's up, Kenny?"

"Keith, we've got some stuff here that should be brought to your attention"

"Like what?"

Winthrop stood quietly in the corner, listening to every word that Lang imparted about securing the search warrant and discovering what they found in the house. While Lang described the scene to Winthrop, Lauren noticed another item that raised a great deal of concern.

"Ah, man," Lang said upon seeing the new discovery.

"What?" Winthrop asked.

"You're not going to believe what Lauren just found," Lang said almost in disbelief.

"All right," Winthrop said. "When you finish that up meet me back at headquarters."

****

As Lang dropped his jacket and paperwork down in the chair situated next to his desk, Winthrop came marching in, his necktie loosened and sleeves rolled up.

"I've got her in room number two if you want to watch the interview," Winthrop said. "If she starts coming up with a bunch of bullshit that needs to be run down, I'll need you to run it down before she leaves the room. It won't do us any good to have her run and tell everyone what she told us before we can interview them."

"You got it," Lang said and began making his way towards the monitoring room.

Tossing his notepad onto an ancient gray desk, Lang situated himself into the chair, kicked his feet up, and placed the headphones over both ears to avoid being distracted by other detectives who would be coming in and out of the room to get an update on the latest homicide case.

Tweaking the volume knob, Lang found the most comfort he could in the confined office quarters.

Doris was already seated in the room. As she tapped her fingernails on the wooden table, causing a sharp piercing echo in the headset, Lang found the ambient noise irritating. The clatter of the door announced Keith was entering the room as the monitor revealed him closing the door and taking a seat next to Doris Riley.

"Doris, thanks for coming up here today. I realize that this must be a pretty stressful day for you," he said.

"Yes it has been," she answered trying to manufacture some tears.

"Before we get too far into this conversation, I'm hungry. Would you like some pizza if I order one?"

"Oh, yes," she answered, flattered by the invitation.

Within the interview room, Detective Winthrop made the call and arranged for a pepperoni pizza to be delivered to the two from the local Domino's Pizza.

"You don't like anchovies do you?" he asked, slightly pulling the phone away from his ear.

"Oh, no," she answered.

"Nope. No anchovies, just pepperoni on that pizza, Champ," he said to the pimply faced kid on the other end of the line.

Hanging up his cell phone, Winthrop straightened the blank legal pad on the desk in front of him and dropped his ink pen right in the middle of the tablet. Lacing his fingers atop of his head, he leaned back in the chair and recounted the events Doris had conveyed to him earlier in the family room.

"Is that an accurate representation of what we talked about at the hospital?" he asked, knowing the digital video recorder was capturing every nuance of the interview.

"Yes, you got it right," she said, somewhat pleased, with a hint of giddiness.

"Doris, there are some things we need to talk about. While I was at the hospital with you today, another detective was at your house," he revealed, slowly measuring her countenance. "And that detective's job is to process the death scene when someone dies. So because Stevie died in the house, we take our crime lab over and look for evidence to support your account of what happened."

"Can you do that?" she asked with some concern.

"Yes, we can. You see, that detective applied for a search and seizure warrant which explained to the judge the circumstances of Stevie's death. The judge signed the search warrant, authorizing us to go into your house and search for anything that may pertain to Stevie's death. Do you understand?" Winthrop asked.

Folding her hands in her lap, Doris nodded and whispered she understood.

"So, we've been in your house and have had the opportunity to see a lot of stuff. Is there anything you'd like to tell me?" Winthrop posed.

"I can't think of anything to tell you," she said calmly, with certain resolute in her eye.

"Doris, we've been in your basement, seen your computer. Let's start there."

"Okay, so? You've seen my computer. What does that have to do with anything?" she asked.

"What were you looking at on the Internet, Doris?" Winthrop asked, hoping to invoke some explanation on her behalf.

"Cruises. Big deal," she retorted.

"They cost a lot of money, don't they?" Winthrop posed.

"Yeah, so?"

"How did you plan on paying for that cruise, Doris?"

"Overtime from Fred's paycheck. We'd like to go to the Bahamas for our five-year anniversary," she added.

"How much do you have saved towards this cruise?"

"Nothing."

"And when's your anniversary?"

"In two and a half months." she said.

"And you have nothing saved up to pay for this trip?"

"Nope. What's this got to do with Stevie?" she asked, trying to turn the tables on the seasoned detective.

Winthrop paused, knowing that playing into her hand would only frustrate the situation. Either she knew he was on to her game or she was just too stupid to comprehend. Winthrop hadn't decided which of the two she was, but if she was just too stupid, he knew he was in for a very long night.

Timing the pizza delivery boy almost to the minute, Winthrop stepped out from the room and returned a few moments later with the piping hot pizza box, two cans of sodas, and paper towels.

"You hungry?" he asked.

"You, bet," Doris answered exuberantly.

"Here you go!"

Winthrop laid the box on the table and slid the cola can towards Doris. Ripping off a piece of paper towel, he placed a slice of pizza on the towel and served his guest.

"Thank you," she replied with extreme gratitude.

Winthrop was already considering his next move. The move that would help reveal just what kind of person with whom he was dealing. Cracking open his can of cola, Winthrop grabbed a slice of pizza and initiated his next move, which comprised of nothing at all. He decided he would play a little head game with Doris. He would sit quietly in the room, ask her nothing, and avoid making any eye contact with her. She seemed interested in him enough earlier. He felt certain that Doris would feel compelled to say something over dinner. Most women did. As he took his second bite of the pepperoni pizza, Winthrop swiveled his chair to point away from Doris and stared into the antique white abyss fixed on the plain drab wall.

"Wow," she said just minutes after Winthrop initiated his game of silence. "I've got a fresh hot pizza and a handsome detective with me. This is the best day of my life!"

Winthrop fought back the urge to make any movement, to neither quicken nor slow his chewing pace, to give no indication about how her statement had infuriated him. *Her son is dead and this is the best day of her life? What the hell?* Winthrop gnawed on a piece of chewy crust. Taking a sip of soda, Winthrop flipped open the box lid, pulled out another piece, and turned towards Doris.

"Want another slice of pizza?"

CHAPTER FIFTEEN

The hours had been grueling. Sifting through the events of the day and only getting little pieces of information at a time left Winthrop wondering if Doris intentionally killed her son. Having slipped out of the interview room, the detective found himself standing at his desk, pouring through the pile of paperwork that had been generated while dining with his guest. As Doris was probably pulling her third piece of pie from the grease-stained cardboard box, Winthrop threw the reports, scattering them across his desk in utter frustration.

"I don't get it," he said to anyone who would listen. "How does a mother just get up one morning and decide 'Hey, today I think I'll kill my son!'. Can anyone tell me how that happens?"

"You don't think she did it?" a detective from the three-to-eleven shift asked.

"I don't know! Lang found all this shit at the house that makes things look bad, but she's pretty adamant that she was downstairs on the computer surfing the web."

"Did you go at her yet with the circumstantial evidence?" asked the detective.

"I'm not sure I want to, yet; I'd hate to go at her and find out at the autopsy tomorrow that the kid must have had some bona fide medical issue that no one knew about."

"What's your gut tell you?" asked the detective.

The question stopped Winthrop dead in his thoughts. He hadn't stepped back and looked at the big picture just yet, he only had the opportunity to speak with the family and go off of the information that Lang just relayed to him. Nothing Lang said gave indication of a fresh murder, a new attack on this day, but the information was overwhelmingly stacked against the mother.

"You're right," Winthrop acknowledged as he grabbed a fresh pack of Marlboro Lights and stormed out of the squad room.

****

The solid wood door abruptly slammed shut as Winthrop turned his chair around and straddled the seat. Smacking one end of the unopened pack of cigarettes against the palm of his hand, he ripped the cellophane off from around the cardboard box and placed a freshly tampered cigarette between his lips.

"We have some issues we need to talk about," Winthrop said as Doris' eyes became enticed by the glowing embers dancing at the ends of his lips.

Winthrop drew in a deep breath, holding in his breath as he gave the mother a cold hard stare, and then exhaled the smoke, directly into her face, enticing her even more.

"Can I have one?" she asked, hers eyes revealing the truth of her longing to satisfy her craving.

"First, we need to talk about some problems," Winthrop said as he closed the box and placed it into his shirt pocket where it would silently tempt the addict.

"Like what?" she asked.

"There's this whole issue with the popcorn and ice cream bowls lying around the house," he said, drawing another long drag while offering another cold hard stare.

"Stevie likes to eat popcorn and ice cream when he's watching cartoons. So?"

"At 8:30 in the morning?" Winthrop snapped.

"And what's wrong with—"

"What's wrong with that?" Winthrop continued on his rant. "I don't know about you, but the rest of the world has cereal in the morning! You know! Cheerios! Fruit Loops! Apple Jacks! Not this French vanilla ice cream shit topped with Orville Redenbacher's movie night popcorn! Don't you fix him anything to eat? Or does he have to feed himself?"

"I feed my boy just fine," Doris said scolding her accuser.

"Like what? What did you fix for him last night for dinner?"

"A peanut butter and jelly sandwich," she exclaimed folding her arms.

"That's it? A peanut butter and jelly sandwich? And I suppose you gave him some barbeque chips with that too!"

"So what if I did?" she retorted.

"He's four years old! What about making him some chicken and vegetables? You know—something healthy," he said in a calmer, fatherly voice.

"If you're trying to say I'm not a good mother, you've got it wrong," she countered

Winthrop caught the sudden employment of her defensive tactics; he had seen this a hundred times in the box. *I'll have to take it slow with her.* He sat back in his chair, allowing the silence to create space as he logically prepared the order in which he would begin picking her story apart.

****

She sat muted in the corner of the room, fuming as she weighed the audacity the detective had in confronting her with his fruitless allegation. *Tell me I don't feed my kid! Who the hell does he think he is?* The words nearly fell of the edge of her lips as her eyes glared at her opponent. Then, almost without warning, memories of happier times raced through her mind as the realization nothing would ever be the same became a haunting reality in her life. *I can't tell him! I can't tell him anything. Nobody, not even my husband knows.*

Winthrop perceived the uneasy mood now emanating from his potential prisoner. Her long drawn look confirmed for him

160

he was venturing down a path she hoped could have been avoided. Perched in his chair with a shrewd grin on his face, Winthrop sat vigilant, letting the deafening silence of the room engulf her like a dark shadow from a fiery abyss.

"Let's talk about what we found upstairs," Winthrop said, piercing the stillness, giving a gruff look from the corner.

"Which closet?" she snapped, her arms still folded across her chest.

"The one in your bedroom." he said leaning in towards her.

"What about it?"

"You tell me!"

"There's nothing to tell!"

"Really? Then explain to me why there is a pile of clothes pushed down onto the floor, much like a bird's nest, with a box of chips and pretzels, and a small television sitting on a table right in front of the door," he insisted.

"So? That's how I store my stuff," she replied in desperation.

"Your stuff? YOUR STUFF?" he screamed. "You mean your four-year old son, don't you?"

"I don't know what you're—"

"Liar!" he said leaping to his feet, leaning over the table, and pointing his finger directly into her face. His face flaring blood red from the anger raging through his veins, Winthrop unloaded on her with everything he had.

"I'll tell you exactly what that closet is for! That closet isn't for storing your stuff! That's Stevie's 'timeout corner,' isn't it? That's where Stevie goes when he's been a bad boy! That's the place you put him when he's pestering you, getting on your nerves, when you can't take it anymore. That's what that is!"

Doris' eyes suddenly welled up with tears. She hadn't expected this. Squinting her eyes and bowing her head, she hoped the perceptive detective hadn't noted her sudden loss of emotion control. *Keep it together girl.* Taking in another deep breath, *No one knows.*

Without missing a beat, Winthrop kept his quickened tempo, drumming on the hard cold evidence the investigators located at the house. Unrelenting, he continued his rampage.

"It's Stevie's little cell! You toss his ass in there when you get tired of him, when he gets on your nerves, when he's interrupting your Internet time! You throw his ass in there, leave him in the dark, and to be sure that he doesn't get out, you wedge the screw driver under the door, don't you?"

Doris' eyes darted straight at the detective. Hatred festered in her like she had never experienced.

Winthrop continued, "Then, when he's been in there a few hours, he starts knocking on the door, promising he'll be good. So you come and open the door, throw in a Barney DVD and tell him he has to finish his timeout! Stevie's little chamber, a place you can put him and be left alone."

"It's where he plays while I'm cleaning the—"

"Cleaning what? The house? Because if you're talking about *your* house I'll tell you now that it hasn't seen a dust rag or vacuum in years! Don't give me that bullshit!"

Winthrop sat back down in his chair, allowing another calculated hush to fall over the room. Following a precise interval of time, Winthrop continued with a small reverent voice, "We found the empty bowls with the popcorn and ice cream specials he'd make, the closet you'd lock him in, *and—* the blood stains at the bottom of the basement steps."

Doris froze, a void sank deep into her chest as she allowed the last statement to resonate within her. *Did he just say blood stains?* Rubbing her hands on the tops of her legs, Doris' eyes violently twitched from side to side as she thought about how she would explain away the blood stains.

"Stevie... Stevie was clumsy. He was always falling down," she offered in a soft whisper. "If you look at him you'll see bruises all over him from where he was falling down. In fact, just the other day he fell down the basement steps and bloodied his nose."

The case was slowly falling apart right before Winthrop's eyes. She countered every charge that he laid before her with some rational explanation that, undoubtedly, some idiotic juror would potentially buy in a criminal trial. And he knew he didn't even have enough evidence to bring any formal charges against her, though his gut was telling him she was an abusive mother whose actions ultimately led to his death. Winthrop sat uneasy as he determined his next logical maneuver.

"We have some witnesses you know?" he posed.

"Witnesses for what?"

"What happened this morning?"

"Nothing happened this morning!" she said with all confidence.

"Really? What about the thumping up and down the stairs?"

"It's Tuesday." she said "I do laundry on Tuesdays."

"And just you and Stevie were home?"

"It's always just Stevie and me during the day."

****

Early morning sunbeams glistened off of the rippling water, slapping against the concrete wall along the Inner Harbor, its sparkles refracted against the polished glass high-rises. Doctor Abdullah parked his Mercedes, scanned his card, and entered the side door to the medical examiner's building. It would be a busy morning, as a handful of autopsies came in late afternoon the day prior. With just enough time to grab the roll call sheet and a cup of coffee, Doctor Abdullah made his way into the basement, around the corner and into the cool, stale autopsy room.

"Good morning, Doc," Winthrop called out already standing by the gurney bearing the four-year olds remains.

"Good morning, Detective. What brings you downtown, today?" the physician asked.

"This four year old," he said nodding with his head. "Mom found him unconscious on the living room couch."

"Doing what?" the doctor asked.

"Watching cartoons, eating popcorn and ice cream," Winthrop said.

Dr. Abdullah looked at the detective with a bewildered look. "And nothing suspicious?"

"We talked to one neighbor who says she heard a repeated

thumping noise going down the steps. When I talked to mom, she denied any wrong-doing and said she does laundry on Tuesdays," Winthrop said shrugging his shoulders.

The physician cocked his head as his attention diverted to the stark naked body lying on the gurney. Most of the skin had already begun to ashen from the onset of lividity. Dr. Abdullah caught a glimpse of yellow across the mid-torso of the cadaver.

"Look here," he said pointing, "see how this is yellow and oval? Now look over here. This one is similar in shape, but purple in color. Both are bruises caused by similar trauma, but inflicted on the young boy at two different periods in time."

"That's the problem, Doc. She says the boy is clumsy and falling down all the time. I'm not so sure. Unless you have definitive proof to say otherwise, I'm not sure how you're going to rule on this death," Winthrop said.

Dr. Abdullah looked down the row of twenty–three gurneys each having its own medical investigation awaiting. With a deep sigh of resignation, the doctor looked up at Winthrop and insured him he would personally oversee this autopsy.

"Do you have any crime scene photos?" the doctor asked.

"Back at the office," Winthrop answered.

"Email them to me; I'll see what I can do." And with this last instruction, Dr. Abdullah turned to the next gurney, picked up the chart and started what was to be a very long day.

****

Cornering himself on the first floor, the crazed lunatic held two family members at bay with a cleaver. The deranged look emanating from his dark, hollow eyes gave every indication no level of help would resolve his issue. Today, someone was going to die.

"Look, Roger," the elderly man pleaded with his grandson. "Just put the knife down and no one will get hurt."

The six-foot-four Neanderthal swung around, clenching the cleaver's handle so tightly that his bare white knuckles could be seen from across the room. Glaring from behind his ringing wet nappy hair, the tormented soul gave a scouring look at his captives as he gritted his teeth and groaned as if speaking in an unknown tongue.

"Roger, just calm down. We're not doing anything to you," the old man said, swallowing hard. "Just put the knife down. You're making Grandpa nervous. Please."

Roger's delirium came from a long road of misdirection and bad decisions. His mother didn't think marijuana abuse in middle school was that big of an infraction. But later, after her sudden and unexpected death, Roger, who never knew the identity of his father, was raised by his grandparents. . Only they were unable to control his insatiable hunger for more addictive cosmic drugs that often set him in a delirium with fits of rage. Escaping the realities of his life, Roger found a whole new world, one in which he made achievements:, when he smoked his marijuana laced with LSD that is.

From his seated position in the faded blue recliner, Mr. Clark pulled his cell phone from his pocket, flipped it open, and held down the speed dial feature for 911. *I pray they'll hear what's going on and send someone out!* With a quick glance, Mr. Clark saw the call connected as he turned off the speaker phone feature and then turned down the volume. Roger would go ballistic if he knew.

"911, what is your emergency?" the operator asked not receiving a response.

Repeating the question only brought about similar results. Tapping his headset, he turned up the volume on the console and concentrated on the background noise. He had handled several calls in the past where callers were unable to directly speak to the 911 operator due to the plight they were in and needed immediate help. Within seconds, the operator could distinctly hear one voice yelling and another, pleading to put the knife down. Signaling his supervisor to the call, the communications center activated their exigency plan for wireless carriers, pinpointing the exact geographical location of the cell phone, within three feet, within ninety seconds. *Technology has come a long way in the past fifteen years.* Having the coordinates, the duty sergeant sounded the alert tones, and

STANDING IN DEATH'S SHADOW

dispatched uniformed officers to the 'unknown trouble' on Berkley Road.

"All units, be advised, one subject is armed with a knife and may have hostages." The radio squelched.

Mr. Clark sat calmly in his chair, repeatedly pleading with his grandson to put down the knife. As a faint high-pitched squeal rang in his left ear, Mr. Clark reached up and twisted the miniscule knob on the hearing device plugged in his ear. As the squealing increased and became clearer, Mr. Clark realized his covert plan had worked and police with sirens blaring were now making their way to his bungalow home. As Roger tuned into the approaching police sirens, Mr. Clark folded his phone, closing the connection to 911, and covertly returned the phone to his pocket.

Running to the front picture window and throwing back the curtains, Roger saw the first patrol car pull up in front of the residence and he bellowed a roar that neither of his grandparents had ever heard before.

****

The two seasoned officers were tactful in how they determined their approach to the house. When their directed phone call from the stationhouse into the residence failed, one officer retrieved the twenty-gauge shotgun, chambered a round, and flipped the safety off as the two approached the side kitchen door. When they were within twenty feet of reaching the door, Roger framed himself in the door, cleaver in hand, and told the officers if they didn't get off the property he would begin butchering his grandparents.

The announcement of the 'barricade' over the police radio immediately ignited a series of events that would continue until the situation was ultimately resolved. With a force of some 1800 well trained officers, law enforcement officials had no intention of backing down. In fact, they would resolve the situation on their terms with no exceptions.

The mobile command post deployed and took up residence at the local firehouse just three blocks from the target location.

Uniformed officers set up a perimeter and evacuated the neighbors without drawing any undo rampages from Roger, who verbally disapproved of their presence. Hostage negotiators scrambled from the far corners of the county, dropping their current activities and racing to the staging area just a few miles off the I-95 interstate. Likewise, the day work SWAT team, who had just finished a five-mile run, changed from their PT gear into their olive drab jumpsuits and then soared down the highway; their strobe lights flickering at a frantic pace as their sirens screamed for civilians to 'make way.'

With various resources converging upon the command post simultaneously, Commander Martin took the reigns and gave firm direction.

"I want the Hostage Negotiation Team to try to establish communications with our boy inside the house while SWAT deploys their snipers." Pulling up an overhead satellite image of the residence on an oversized computer screen, a support officer zoomed out from the residence to allow the SWAT team officers to scope out snipers' nests that would provide maximum coverage while avoiding any potentially deadly crossfire or collateral damage.

"I'll take this corner; you go here," the one sniper said to the other. "If we can get into the second floor of this house," he said pointing to the screen, "it should give me a clean shot if I need it."

The sergeant surveyed the bird's-eye view of the target location and the locations selected to set up the high-powered rifles. With a nod of approval, the snipers deployed while HNT made the required connections to setup their portable communication center.

"Just a few more minutes, Major, and we should be up and running," the lead tech officer indicated.

As the officer predicted, the equipment sprang to life, chirping and blinking, giving all indication to the command staff that when they were ready, a negotiator could place the call and hopefully, with some persistent skill, talk everyone out of the house.

****

Entering the sixth hour of the standoff, tensions mounted, both within the residence and the mobile command post. Major Martin had activated each of the units with a great deal of precision; HNT was talking to the guy, SWAT had positioned their snipers, who where feeding intelligence back into the command post, and medics were standing by just in case the worst unfolded. But, now that the command post was bustling with all the upper brass, the colonels and the chief himself, Martin's control was usurped as the egotistical higher ranking commanders now argued and debated their next move.

"He's only talking to the negotiator every now and then," the colonel indicated.

"Yes, but he's still talking, sir," Martin replied.

"Right now he's in control of this situation and not us! Tell SWAT they need to suit up, we're sending them in," the colonel barked.

"But Colonel—"

"But nothing! During the past six hours, this guy has only become more agitated and more prone to violence. I don't need him butchering his grandparents while we're sitting out here with our thumbs up our ass. Send in SWAT and let's neutralize the situation, Major."

"Yes, sir," came the soft-spoken acknowledgement.

****

"Okay, boys, because both snipers are deployed, we'll only have six on the stick," the sergeant said as the group of former special forces experts huddled around the front of his car.

"Sarge, it'll be dusk in about three hours. Any chance of waiting so we can move under the cover of darkness?" asked the former Navy Seal.

"Nope. Colonel wants us in there yesterday. The plan is to snake down the block a street over from the target location. Once we've reached house number 531, we'll cut up through their yard and straight into the right side of the target location.

There's a bush that should give us some cover, but as you know, we're out here in broad daylight, so we need to move fast. Johnston, you'll be point-man with the bunker. Miller, you're on the ram… any questions?" The sergeant surveyed the officers and from the look in each man's eyes, was confident that each knew his assignment. "Very good, let's go."

Each of the six men doubled up with his partner and completed their weapons check followed by a radio check. Johnston lifted the fifty-pound bulletproof shield and led the way up the narrow side street with the rest immediately behind him in single file forming the stick. Johnston saw the house number, his cue to make his turn, leading the stick up through the yard, across the street and directly into the targets yard just as planned.

"Sniper Two, I have the team in sight. They made it into the target's yard unchallenged." chirped the radio.

Jones crept quietly along the side of the house until he reached the back corner where he intended to pause, giving the team one last moment before breaching the premises and engaging their nemesis.

"Sniper One, I have the team in sight. No activity on my side of the residence." The radio squelched and chirped.

Johnston turned around and faced his team. "We'll have to circle the front porch and line straight up with the front door for the breach. After Miller rams the door, we're going in, banking right, and clearing one room at a time. Edwards, get to the foot of the stairway, that cover the room on the left and the stairs until we clear the first floor. Ready? On my count…"

Sniper One saw the momentary pause in the offensive assault, knowing last minute assignments were being given now that the boys had a chance to better assess their target. *Better scope the front side one more time before they deploy.* He raised the scope back to his eye. Scanning across the second floor attic windows, Sniper One noticed no change in the curtainless windows, their silhouettes remaining precisely the same as his last scan. Circling his rifle lower, he was scanning back along the bottom of the house when a shadow caught his eye.

"What the hell was that?" he asked concentrating his sights

169

on the sidelight curtain as it delicately waved once again. The sudden shift of the shadow announced the opening of the front door.

"Sniper One to Team One, stand down, I say again, stand down! Front door is opening!"

The expert rifleman pulled the stock in tightly to his shoulder, repositioned his cheek, shoring up his sight alignment on the front door as the six foot burly figure appeared, the cleaver still clinched in his hand.

"The suspect is in the doorway! Suspect is in the doorway!" Sniper One dispatched over the secured channel.

In one fluid motion, Sniper One deactivated the safety and firmly wrapped his finger around the trigger. Only three pounds away from sending a deadly projectile towards its target, Sniper One consciously initiated his deep breathing exercises, ensuring a one sure and steady shot. Sighting up the crosshairs of his scope directly in the middle of the suspect's head, Sniper One activated his push to talk button one last time.

"Sniper One to Command Post. I've acquired the suspect. What are your orders?"

The radio hissed with silence. Undoubtedly, the new and updated information caused a stir of debate amongst the commanders within the safety of the command post.

"Sniper One to Command Post. I've acquired the—"

In a fraction of a second, the suspect's head vanished from his scope.

Oh shit! Where'd he go?

Opening both eyes, he retraced the suspect, who was now trotting down the front porch steps. Realizing the inherent danger as the suspect was now aggressively heading towards his unsuspecting team members; Sniper One reacquired his target in the scope.

He's too fast for a head shot! Instinctively lowering the rifle towards the madman's torso, he squeezed off the shot and prayed.

Assessing his shot through his scope, Sniper One wasn't sure if the suspect had stumbled or if his round had found its target. Focusing in through the lenses, he could see bright red frothy fluid pouring from the suspect's ribcage. *Bull's-eye!*

"Sniper One to command post," he said, his voice more relaxed, "Shots fired. Suspect is down. Start the medic to the scene."

CHAPTER SIXTEEN

Flipping on the switch and pulling the overhead light down lower to examine his preliminary findings, the doctor leaned in for a closer look. *These bruises are very peculiar.* Taking in their overall oval shape, he pressed in, raising his glasses off his nose, which was so close that it nearly brushed against the cadaver. Upon closer inspection, he could faintly see a darker straight edge running through the center of the bruise. Raising his bushy eyebrow in question, Dr. Abdullah reached over to the manila envelope that had been placed on the gurney by an associate some hours earlier. Bending the tabs and unfolding the flap, he extracted the eight by ten-inch glossy photographs and flipped through them in rapid succession. His sagging eyes wildly scanning each photo before turning to the next, the doctor's quick pace came to an abrupt halt when he flipped one more photo. With a small shift of his bifocals, the doctor's curiosity heightened as he twisted the picture to align it with the small framed body lying before him.

It is very possible. He grabbed the yardstick lying across the boy's legs from the preliminary height measurements. Laying the rule across the first abrasion, he noted the measurement; "0.75 of an inch," he recorded onto the chart. Moving on to the next bruise, he repeated his study. "Very interesting," he said aloud, drawing attention from his assistant standing nearby.

"What's that, Doc?" asked the assistant.

"I believe I have found the cause of death."

****

Having watched the slain beast fall just feet away from where they were hunkered down, the tactical stick made their way around the dead man and entered the unguarded house to search for any other potential threats that had not yet been discovered.

"Clear!" the cry came from the upstairs bedroom.

"Clear!" another came from the kitchen in back.

"Are you folks all right?" the brawny officer asked while letting his MP5 machine gun swing free to his side.

"Yes, we're fine," answered the grandfather in a crackling voice. "But what about my grandson? What has happened to him?"

Secured in a nearby place to stand by until SWAT team members confirmed the scene was safe, the paramedics waited patiently for the "all clear." When the radio transmission came through, the medic unit jumped into action and wheeled around the corner. Both paramedics sprung from their seats, grabbed their gear, and made haste to their patient.

"No pulse or respiration. He's dead." the medical lieutenant announced.

Mr. and Mrs. Clark had emerged onto their chipped concrete porch just in time to see two officers draping the white sheet over their grandson's lifeless body.

"Roger? ROGER!" Mr. Clark exclaimed, cupping his hand around his mouth in horror.

Another set of uniformed officers intercepted the old man, preventing him from embracing his dead grandson and contaminating the scene before crime lab officials had an opportunity to forever memorialize the barricade's outcome with their digital cameras.

"Sir, he's dead, he was going after our officers," explained the patrolman.

"But he wouldn't hurt anyone," interjected the grandmother. "He was such a nice boy."

****

"Yes, Detective, I have made a decision on the cause and manner in the Riley case," said the doctor matter of factly. "I was able to count a total of thirteen contusions on various parts of the boy's body. None were in the same location, which gives me reason to believe the same mechanism of injury wasn't necessarily inflicted in the same manner. Also, when closely inspecting each of these contusions, each exhibited different colors. Some are purplish-black, some reddish-blue, and others are yellow-green; a sure indicator of different stages of healing which confirms that each were inflicted at different times."

Winthrop sat speechless on his end of the phone as his pen etched out his notes in bold black ink. *For crying out loud, Doc, is it a murder or what?*

"In my examination I did find one common characteristic that was similar with each of these contusions. Each of these bruises reflects a linear bruise measuring three-quarters of an inch in thickness. While these striations are consistent in size and positioning with the overall oval shape of the contusions, I couldn't help but notice in your photographs how the basement steps are not carpeted. So I took a little field trip to the local hardware store and found that the edge of the wooden steps on prefabricated steps measure precisely three-quarters of an inch. The rounded edges explain both the displacement of the contusions' color and the—"

"Okay, Doc, I get it. So is it a murder or accidental death?" Winthrop begged over the phone, longing to satisfy the question.

"The injuries and the pattern in which they are exhibited are consistent with repeated abuse over a course of time, Detective. This is a classic case of child abuse where the victim ultimately succumbed to his internal injuries, which was just the case in this death. This is a homicide, Detective, plain and simple."

Winthrop reared back in his chair, relief pouring over him that his gut instinct had been correct. *Will it be enough?* He weighed the lack of evidentiary facts in this case. *Cold hard facts are what the jurors like to see.* And with that thought tearing through his mind, he grabbed the telephone receiver, and dialed the four-digit extension.

****

"Close the door and have a seat," Sergeant Bennett said to the detective walking into his office.

"What's up, Sarge?" Metzger asked.

"Oh, I think you know, Metzger. Can you explain to me why this report is laying on my desk?" Bennett asked, leaning back in his chair with utmost confidence.

Metzger became unnerved, hunching over in his seat as his mind raced through the possible scenarios that now brought him into this uncomfortable position before his superior. His mind first took him to the pub in Ellicott City and the drink-fest that had spawned a manner of conduct that would have been considered unacceptable in most professional circles. But that off-duty episode wouldn't have caused him to generate a report. Then he recalled his recent trip to the next county, while on-duty, relaying some hunting equipment to his cousin who was leaving the next morning for a bear hunt out in the Midwest. But that too wouldn't cause him to generate any paperwork. *What the hell is he talking about?* Lifting his hands in surrender Metzger said, "I'm not sure what you're talking—"

"The Ralph Sullivan case! The one you said you were doing your own surveillance on," Bennett snapped as he flung forward and gripped the edge of his desk.

Oh yeah, that case. "So, what's the problem?" Metzger asked.

"Are you kidding me?" Bennett snatched the supplemental report from his desk and crinkled it in his shaking fist. "This report says you came in this past Saturday and sat down on the house by Clifton Park to see if you could get any tag numbers. Problem is, you weren't there!"

Metzger silently retraced his steps, knowing the integrity accusation that was about to accost him. Leaning forward and folding his hands together, Metzger hung his head as he searched for the right answer to help defuse the situation, negate the charges, and leave him in the best possible position. *Deny the allegation, offer counter charges.*

"I just drove by the location to see if there were any cars, then I—"

"Well check this out, Sherlock! I got to the residence just a little before 1:00 and parked across the street in the church parking lot, and at no time during the subsequent four hours did I see you or your car, drive by the location, which was the whole purpose in you taking the car home over the weekend. Remember that?"

"Sarge, I—"

"I don't want to hear it, Metzger! You came and asked me if you could take the car home over the weekend 'cause you wanted to come in on Saturday and try to get those tag numbers. Then you pull this shit—filing paperwork like you actually did something in the investigation. What the hell were you thinking?" Bennett tossed the reports across his desk and rocked back in his chair as sheer silence pervaded the room.

Metzger sat up, prepared to offer a response, but before he could utter a syllable, Bennett was lashing out again.

"You weren't thinking, Metzger!" Bennett seethed.

"I must have accidentally—" Metzger offered.

"You must have *accidentally* my ass! I came in this morning and not only did I find a completed supplemental report, but you also had the audacity to fill out overtime slips. Rob, I sat down there on that parking lot for four hours; here's your list of tags," the sergeant said, tossing an opened notebook bearing the Maryland registration plates he had secured. "I've had enough of you. Pack your shit. Effective tomorrow you're temporarily reassigned to the Economic Crimes Squad until Internal Affairs finishes this investigation. You're no longer a part of the Homicide Unit. Now get your sorry ass out of my office!"

176

With a careful and steady hand, Lauren depressed the plunger, emptying the fluid from the wide syringe into the sterile test tube. Plugging the opened end of the syringe into the test-tube, she squeezed the plunger, secured it, grabbed another, and repeated the process. Her blue plastic tray, now filled with a handful of test tubes containing a hot wax bath solution was ready. Lauren pulled the clear glass door open on the large gray unit standing in the corner of the lab and placed the small blue tray into its position as she initiated the process to vortex the solution. Re-securing the glass door with the utmost of care, Lauren peered in past her reflection as she entered the codes and activated the unit.

The process would take a precise amount of time before she could retrieve the vortexed solutions and transfer them into a fresh batch of sterile test tubes. Her eyes were becoming dry and fatigued from pressing on hour after hour, but Lauren pushed herself to finish the processing and establish the necessary sequencing that would inevitably yield an answer if the blood found at the bottom of the steps was actually Stevie's.

When she finished jumping the last hurdle, Lauren sat on the stool next to the lab table, cupped her hands over her face to cover her yawn and allowed her mind to drift off into a dark and dampened basement in a row home lost in the populace of the concrete buildings and red brick mortared homes. As a mother herself, she couldn't imagine the cold blood running through such heartless veins that would compel any mother to repeatedly propel their child down a set of stairs, over and over and over again. Her heart sank deep into her chest as her mind contrived images of the tangled four-year old plummeting down the stairs and landing in a limp heap only to be grabbed by the back of his neck, dragged up the stairs and tossed again.

Tears streamed gently down her cheek, dripped onto the tabletop and pulled her thoughts away from the gaunt lifeless eyes of the limp child back to the sequence of data that was nearly completed. Swiping both hands across her cheeks, ensuring her mascara hadn't smudged, Lauren sprang up from the stool and opened the components door and retrieved the final analysis. Taking her place cards and lining them up to inspect the fluorescent marker, Lauren carefully measured each marker looking for the likenesses and differences that would ultimately determine the fate of a mother.

Letting an exasperated sigh escape from the strains of the day, Lauren picked up the phone and dialed the number to the Homicide unit.

"Katherine, its Lauren. Is Detective Winthrop around?"

"Hold on Lauren, Hon. Let me get him for you. He's been expecting your call."

The biologist mentally sorted through the DNA hurdles she had taken this day as she waited on her end of the line and double-checked to ensure nothing was missed. Just as she had confirmed with herself her findings would be validated, Detective Winthrop's gruff voice broke the static silence as he greeted his caller.

"What can you tell me, Lauren?"

"Well, the test still needs to be validated by my supervisor, but I can tell you with all certainty the blood at the bottom of the basement is Stevie's. You have any idea why she would do this?" Lauren asked, still struggling with the concept.

"I hate to say it, but she was on the computer trying to book a cruise for her and her husband's wedding anniversary, and neither of them can afford it... unless they cashed in on the brand new $24,000 life insurance policy Lang found upstairs in their bedroom in Stevie's name."

"That's horrible! I don't understand—how could a mother do that to her child?"

"It gets worse," the seasoned detective said, holding back no reservations. "They had a one-year-old who died last year. The ME ruled it SIDS, but with Stevie's death, we've pulled the case out and have started going over it with a fine tooth comb. So far, it looks just like this one."

****

178

Slumped over the edge of the bar, he glared at the frosty ice-cold mug of his favorite pale ale as his fingers caressed the smooth oblong handle. As the tension of the day's earlier memory spurred back to his conscience the uncertainty of his career, he violently gripped the handle, threw back his head, and chugged the ale in three huge gulps before slamming the mug back onto the bar where it had rested just seconds before. He swiped his fingers across the face of the mug much like a curious child at a frosty windowpane and stared hard at his reflection in the glass. *How'd it come to this?*

Metzger shifted into a straighter position and waved at the bartender.

"Martin. Another Miller Light, please."

One of the most experienced bartenders at The Sideline Tavern, Martin was a looming six and a half-foot tall pale-skinned Irish brut, whose dark hair and barbershop-style mustache gave some hint to his boxing endeavors from his younger days.

"Bad day at the office?" Martin asked, as he replaced the empty mug.

"You could say that," Metzger answered. His glare was focusing on his reflection in the back mirror.

As Metzger sulked in his brew, he felt a familiar and friendly tapping on his shoulder. Turning his head to greet his guest, he found the friendly smile of Sergeant Petrelli greeting him as the sergeant took a seat on the stool beside him.

"Hey, Sarge" Metzger said raising his mug. "Martin. How about a cold one for my friend, here."

"I heard a vicious rumor about you, today. A little birdie tells me that you were kicked out of the homicide unit—any truth to that?"

"It seems that I will be reporting to the Economic Crimes Unit effective tomorrow morning at 0800 hours. Can you believe that? I've busted my ass for twelve years in that hell-hole office, and they kick me out without any formal charges or any trial board," Metzger said.

"Based on what? I mean, what did they say you did that caused you to get kicked out of the unit?"

179

Clasping his ale in both hands, Metzger mused over the question. He certainly couldn't tell a ranking officer of the same agency he had surreptitiously submitted the supplemental report to cover his trail for being hung-over from his Friday night escapades. And to make such admissions would certainly make Sergeant Petrelli a witness in the internal investigation.

"Beats the hell out of me," he finally offered.

"What? They kicked you out of the unit and you don't know why?" Petrelli asked.

"I don't know, since Bennett's been my sergeant, nothing seems to be going right. He won't let me take off as much as I used to and it seems like I'm covering more on call than the other detectives.

Petrelli sat quietly, washing his teeth with his last swig of beer, as Metzger cried his conjectured details about why he was no longer a member of the unit.

Seeing that Petrelli was fully buying into his deception, Metzger continued his rant. "You know, since I've been assigned to Sergeant Bennett, I've had to carry that squad. I mean, really, I've had my hand in every single case on the board. If it wasn't for me, a lot of those cases wouldn't be solved."

"Well, if I were your sergeant, you could count on the fact you would be my number one man and I wouldn't let this kind of bullshit come up in the squad room," Petrelli said angrily as he washed down the last of his beer. "Rob, don't worry about it! If I get assigned to that squad, you can bet that I'll go to bat for you and get you back into the unit ASAP—just hang in there! Oh, and thanks for the beer." Petrelli pushed himself away from the stool and tapped his friend once more on the shoulder he headed for the front door.

Metzger refocused his puzzled look back towards his half-empty mug. He didn't see any other way he could have handled the conversation without involving his friend. To betray his loyalty and arbitrarily offer any information about the drunken frenzy that caused him to miss his surveillance would have certain devastating consequences. Metzger knew he couldn't afford to make any mistakes. He had to be careful about his delicate situation. One slip, one mistake, and termination from his position as a sworn officer would bring irreparable damages. With the dice now rolled, Metzger made his way home and prepared for his first day as a detective chasing down thieves in cyber-world.

CHAPTER SEVENTEEN

The crisp February night air bit through his fleeced denim jacket as he tugged to wrap it around his torso, fighting off the chill that settled deep into his bones. Slinging open the door of his faded blue Ford truck, Charles quickly climbed in and slammed the door shut. As the light from the Old Bay Tavern sign poured in through his windshield, he leaned back against the hardened seat and drew in a long chilled breath. Appreciating the shelter the truck's cab provided from the bite of the winter winds now whipping all around him, Charles rested to gather his senses.

He plunged his hand deep into the warmth of his jacket pocket and retrieved the ice-cold ring of car keys. Finding the appropriate key, Charles aimed for the ignition, but his inebriated state made the task of firing up the truck up and navigating the quarter mile of darkened roadway back to his quaint, two-story cape cod difficult.

Both hands clinched around the steering wheel, Charles huddled forward, and took extra caution along the roadway as he searched for the all too familiar white Chevy Lumina patrol units. They were always easy to see, particularly at night. However, this was a Friday night and he lived in a community that demanded little attention of the local police, which provided Charles with confidence he would make it home without any legal entanglements. He always supported the efforts of the local police officers; it was the nuisance crimes, particularly those that were alleged against him he found to be, well, a nuisance.

As he pulled up in front of the cramped dwelling, he felt the right front tire rub up against the curb, letting him know his massive pickup was far enough to the right to allow other vehicles to freely pass down the narrow street. Charles found that extracting the keys was much easier than when he was in the bar parking lot trying to find the keyhole. *Now, if I can only get the right key in the door.* He leaned against the truck door, pushed it open and staggered towards the kitchen door. Charles was astonished at how quickly he found himself standing in his own kitchen. He grunted as he closed the door and set his keys on the cluttered kitchen table.

The sixty-seven year old telephone company retiree shuffled through the living room where his many hunting and fishing conquests were fondly displayed, adorning every wall. As he clamored through the living room, he tossed his denim jacket onto the edge of the sofa. He rounded the corner and staggered down the hallway into his bedroom. A divorcee with grown children who were now gone and on their own, Charles needn't have any regard for the courtesy of quietness. An avid sportsman, Charles found a great deal of solace in outdoor adventures with his cousin James and his friends at the tavern. Not only were they enthusiasts, but they were accomplished gamesmen with various framed news clippings and trophies littered throughout the house as evidence.

In good bachelor form, Charles kicked off his shoes, doused the light, and fell into his warm cozy bed fully dressed.

****

The modern house once stood as a clapboard schoolhouse in the 1800s but was now entertaining a family who gathered to celebrate a number of February birthdays. The festivities were slated to start at noon. As the family was preparing to take their seats around the two separate tables placed end to end to accommodate all twenty-seven members, Lang poured himself a glass of iced tea as his father cornered him.

"You on call this weekend?" he asked.

"Yeah, but Saturday mornings are usually quiet. Unless, of course, they find someone who died in their sleep the night before and it appears suspicious," Lang said.

"So you shouldn't get called in?"

"Usually on a Saturday morning, I would have already been called out if something is going on. If we get anything it'll probably be later tonight," Lang explained.

As the words fell off the tip of his tongue, Lang felt the pager vibrate on his hip. Lang reached down, depressed the button and observed the comm center's phone number scrolled across the narrow gray screen.

"Aw, come on!" Lang said disappointedly.

"Are they calling you in?" his father asked, grinning.

"Yep. I better see what's going on."

****

Stretching the elastic yellow crime scene tape over his head to enter the secured area, Lang huddled with the rest of the investigative team who were discussing in great length the complexities of the scene that lay just inside the kitchen doorway. Yellow triangle markers were dispensed in numerical order starting on the kitchen floor then trailing through the living room, hallway, master bedroom, bathroom, utility room and out into the back yard. As Lang surveyed the setting, the trail of markers gave all indications the team had an immense task laying before them in determining the last events of their latest victim.

His curiosity now spiked; Lang asked the team the obvious question, "What do we have?"

"The victim's cousin came over around noon today and found him stark naked, lying over the edge of the bathtub. There's a stream of blood coming from his head and going down into the drain. Because of the rifle laying on the edge of the bed, the district guys think it's a suicide, but I'm not buying it," said Carla Brown, the lead forensic technician.

"Well, let's have a look!" Lang said offering a small grin.

Shedding his long coat and suit jacket, Lang pulled elastic gloves onto his hands, grabbed his notebook and made his way up to the side porch door. As he surveyed the door, a small dark smudge caught his eye and drew him in for a closer inspection. Extracting his compact high intensity flashlight, Lang flicked on the beam and leaned in closer to inspect his find.

"Hey, Carla. Did you see this dried blood on the side door?" Lang asked.

"Once you get in there you'll find dried blood everywhere," she said.

"Well, this one looks like it might have a partial fingerprint in it," Lang said.

Cautiously opening the door, Lang stepped into the kitchen area. The bright yellow markers sat meticulously positioned, intending to guide the investigators' path throughout the remainder of the day.

Coin wrappers were strewn across the kitchen floor and a brand new EcoCitizens watch box lay open, revealing missing valuable contents. Inspecting the kitchen with a keen eye, Lang inventoried the contents of the small round table and found several clean spots amongst the cluttered mess that hadn't seen a dust rag in years.

Pulling open the drab green refrigerator door, Lang was overcome with the smell of food in various stages of decay. However, pristine Pabst Blue Ribbon beer cans filled an entire shelf as they waited to be cracked and downed.

When he stepped into the living room area there was evidence in every corner that proclaimed the residence was occupied solely by an avid sportsman. The trophy buck, pair of pheasants, and mounted quail were perfectly situated on each wall. The furniture filled more space than the room offered and was littered with a variety of clothes and afghans that had been placed in certain order.

As Lang lingered around the boundary of the darkened hallway, a warning came from across the small little cottage.

"Be careful. There's a lot of blood in the hallway and I still need to get good close-up pictures f the bloody footprints," cried Carla.

As he peered around the corner into the master bedroom, Lang saw the tiny, muddled room, dominated by a king-sized bed that horded most of the space. With decisive and purposeful steps, Lang crept around the dried blood stains to stand in the doorway of the master bedroom. Much of the décor appeared to be reminiscent of 1966, but this grabbed Lang's attention much less than the stench of unlaundered clothing, reminiscent of the boy's locker room from his high school days.

With exactness, Lang moved into the room and searched every crevice. More bare spots were scattered atop the disheveled bureau and left a few remnants of tools and equipment from days past at the telephone company. The company hard hat with its faded "Telco" logo and work belt sat unscathed where its former owner had placed them a few years ago when he came home from his last day on the job.

As he moved next to the oversized bed, Lang focused his attention on the pillows, sopping wet with dark, congealing blood; only a light amount of blood spatter showed on the overhead ceiling. *I can see why the district guys think it's a suicide.*

Most concerning was the .50 caliber muzzleloader lying on the edge of the bed. With the muzzle pointed towards the headboard and the firing mechanism turned away from where the victim was lying when receiving the deadly blows, Lang questioned whether it was even possible to sustain such an injury and be able to discard the hefty rifle off to the side.

"I think it's a botched suicide," said one uniformed officer, poking his head into the door.

"You think he shot himself with this rifle, then wandered down the hallway into the bathroom and died?" Lang asked.

"I do," he said gripping his gun belt with confidence.

"He couldn't have," Lang said. "If he would have shot himself with that muzzleloader, he would have had to put the barrel in his mouth and there wouldn't be anything left on his shoulders. It would've been sprayed all over the headboard, walls, and ceiling. Plus, I hunt with a muzzleloader. They have a very strong distinctive powder odor when they've been fired, and I don't smell that," Lang countered.

"So, how does he bleed that much in bed and then get to the bathroom?"

"I don't know," Lang confided.

Satisfied with the cursory search in the bedroom, Lang navigated his way down the hallway where a small shiny object caught his eye. *A watch battery?* Lang pondered the various possibilities that might explain how such a tiny component could have been dislodged and found its way to such an unusual location in the middle of the violent torrent.

While he stood in the doorway of the cramped bathroom, Lang studied the pale, lifeless body slung over the edge of the tub just as it was found hours earlier. One arm was draped outside the tub, the other wrapped up around the top of his head which obscured any chance of viewing the wound that bled so profusely. Lang looked over his shoulder, back down the hallway, surmising just how the victim ended up in the bathroom. No obvious answers came to him, so Lang turned, and diverted his attention to unusual blood smears across the bathroom wall.

What the...? Lang backed towards the light switch and linen closet. The smears stretched across the switch, revealing how a bloodied hand reached into the closet, possibly searched for a towel. *I don't get it.* Lang looked across the bathroom, taking in the blood smears across the sink, toilet seat, and bathtub.

"What do you make of it?" Carla asked the puzzled detective.

"I'm not quite sure! Would it even be possible for him to have sustained these injuries, walked into the bathroom and grabbed a towel to try and stop the bleeding?" Lang wondered aloud.

"I don't know. There's a lot of blood on those pillows in the bedroom."

"And there's a lot of blood on the floor between the bedroom and the bathroom. Maybe he did make it here, grabbed a towel, tried to see his injuries at the sink, felt dizzy, sat down on the toilet and then leaned over into the bathtub to wash off his head."

"That's possible. I hadn't thought of that!" Carla offered.

"But then again, like you said, there's a lot of blood on those pillows."

With the remainder of the house still needed searched and processed, the investigative team worked methodically and tediously throughout the remaining portion of the bloodied crime scene. As they neared their conclusion, Sergeant Petrelli flipped open his cell phone, contacted the comm center and forwarded the request for the medical examiner to respond to the scene.

Carla grabbed her toolboxes and camera case as she manipulated the equipment to a new location near the rear of the house; a new partially completed addition stocked with tons of rubbish, which was the next area that needed processed. Old radios, scores of power tools, and crab traps stacked to the ceiling, barely in balance, cluttered the room. There was no clear methodical logic to the organization of the clutter strewn throughout the 625 feet of square footage provided by the outsized room. The only area that afforded any space lay just in front of the French doors that were standing open in spite of the cold February evening air that chilled everyone to the bone.

****

We had been on the scene eleven hours before Carla reviewed her notes and confirmed that, with the exception of the examination of the body by the medical examiner, the scene was processed; the evidence gathered and collected. As the heaping pile of brown evidence bags sat stacked against the far living room wall, Alyson Moore was escorted through the side kitchen door by a uniformed officer.

"The ME is here," the officer announced with some elation, hoping to end the long drawn out day.

As Alyson stepped into the living room and joined the circle of fatigued investigators, she withdrew a thin stainless steel clipboard from her dark brown leather satchel, pulled out a carbonized form from within and clipped it to the front. Lang and Brown huddled with the young and petite medical examiner who sought the preliminary investigation information she needed before she dragged the lifeless body out in front of the television for a more formal examination. After she completed each of her required blocks, Alyson set the clipboard atop her satchel and asked to see the body.

****

Family members flooded the mother's small cottage just down the street from where her son now lay dead, strewn out on a body bag on the living room floor while a host of investigators studied every aspect of his body.

"Detective, would you like something to drink?" the weary, grieving mother offered.

"I'd like a beer, but I'm still on the clock," Gibson offered with a wide humorous grin, breaking the solemn mood, "but a glass of ice water will do."

As Elizabeth started to get up from the kitchen table, one of her grandchildren quickly took over, preparing the glass of ice water for the detective.

"Thank you, Heather," Elizabeth said, "I have a wonderful family you know," she said smiling through her teary eyes. "Charles was such a good boy. I know his marriage didn't work out, but he has some beautiful children who are now all grown up and doing well on their own. I can't imagine anyone wanting to kill my boy," she said, fresh tears streaming down her cheeks.

"Well, I can!" James said sharply.

"Oh, yeah? And who is that?" Gibson asked.

"That damned Jeremy! I'm telling you, if anybody has anything to do with Charles' death, I bet it was him."

"And why is that?" Gibson continued.

"Cause he's the neighborhood asshole. Sorry, Mom, but he is. He's always breaking into people's houses, stealing shit, and pawning it. Probably taking all that money and shooting it up his veins," the angry cousin exclaimed.

"Yeah, but how do you know specifically that he's responsible for your cousin's death?"

"I don't; it's just a gut feeling."

****

Seventeen contorted cadavers silently rested on the dulled gray gurneys that lined the entire distance of the autopsy room when Lang walked in and found Charles' body. With brilliant white fluorescent lights that radiated downwards onto the newly found victims of death's plot, it proved a far better scenario for evaluating Charles' head injuries than the dark and dingy living room the night before.

Lang hovered over the battered bloodshot cranium and closely inspected the damage for any trace of the mechanism that had brought Charles to his sudden demise. There were no prominent, deep purple grooves or patterns that formed; no particularly identifiable outlines; nothing that could be measured and fitted with any given item. Repeated oval trauma ·points, one layered upon the other, culminated to a large portion of the right side of Charles' head being caved in by an unknown object.

"Good morning, Detective Lang. And how are you on this fine blustery morning?" Doctor Abdullah asked, taking note of the detective's efforts.

"I'm well, Doc. Just trying to figure out what was used against my victim's head."

"You don't see any obvious patterns?"

"Not really, but then again, I'm not the expert," Lang said with a wry grin.

"Well then, let's have a look."

After he grabbed a royal blue disposable Bic razor from the supply bins, Dr. Abdullah made haste of shaving off the bloody, knotted hair on the one side of the Charles' head. As the lumps of bloodied hair fell onto the table top, the significant amount of trauma became more apparent to the doctor and detective.

190

Lang turned totally numb as the evidence of hatred unleashed on the small and fragile retiree was unveiled. The deep purple and black bruises that encircled the concaved portion of the head left no doubt that Charles' head was crushed. *Bone fragments must have splintered and shot into his brain, hopefully extending some form of mercy in his dying moments.*

Soon, pity was replaced with anger and anger with a deep personal rage. As trained pathologists ripped and tore into the cadavers all around, Lang's mind drifted to a passage of scripture he always held close to his heart during moments like this.

For rulers hold no terror for those who do right, but for those who do wrong. Do you want to be free from fear of the one in authority? Then do what is right and he will commend you. Lang remembered the words from the book of Romans, the thirteenth chapter. *For he is God's servant to do you good. But if you do wrong, be afraid, for he does not bear the sword for nothing. He is God's servant, an agent of wrath to bring punishment on the wrongdoer.*

Resolved to avenge this monstrous attack, Lang's attention was drawn back to the reality before him. Dr. Abdullah carefully made the incision across the back of the head as he slowly worked the skin free from the skull and pushed the forehead over the victim's face. He pulled an extension cable from its coiled position suspended from the ceiling and plugged in the small circular saw that hummed with a slight squeal as the doctor pressed the rotating blade against the skull and made two cuts. Before the fine dry skull dust had a moment to settle on the floor, Dr. Abdullah grabbed a small metal tool, wedged it into the top lateral cut and gave a firm twist. A loud, solid pop reverberated throughout the room as the top back quarter piece of the skull fell onto the top of the metallic table. Immediately, with no effort exerted by the doctor or his assistant, the brain slid out from the skull cavity in three separate pieces.

"My God," the doctor cried, "I've never seen such trauma! He was so severely beaten that his brain became dislodged from itself. What incredible brutality was exerted against him!"

"Doc, are you seeing any familiar patterns, anything I can

191

look for as a weapon?" Lang asked.

"I can't say. I can tell you it was not an object with a pointy or edged ridge. See, look here," he said lifting the forehead back into place. "This bruise is just one instance where the suspect struck the victim in the head with some sort of rounded blunt object. Here is another—and another—and here are even more."

"How many times was he struck in the head, doc?" Lang asked.

"I could only count twenty-three specific impacts on his head. But, given the level of internal damage, I can say with all certainty that he was struck more than that. Also, look here," the doctor said, drawing the detective's attention to the victim's arms lying by his side. "Do you see the smaller oval sores?"

"Yes. Defensive wounds?"

"Exactly. Look, they are only on the outside of the arms and not on the inside. He was trying to defend himself," the doctor explained as he lifted his arms above his head showing the defensive posture probably exerted by the victim in the initial stages of the attack.

"So when the attacker gets a couple of good blows in, the victim's arms drop and the suspect just keeps beating him."

"Yes, precisely. And given the amount of blood you described at the scene, your victim didn't die instantly. No, I'm afraid he suffered for some time while he was bled."

"With all this trauma, Doc, do you think that he could have walked to the bathroom and tried to treat himself before dying?" Lang asked seeming to believe in light of the severe trauma that the probability was not likely.

"Actually, yes. We have documented cases where victims have experienced such extensive injuries and have survived and been able to move some distance from the spot of their injury. Most, however, are cases of soldiers injured in combat; particularly during World War II. But, nevertheless, it is possible," the doctor said, gazing back at the victim's injuries.

"So I suppose that you're ruling this one a homicide, blunt force trauma?"

"Very good Detective. But be very careful in making

rulings around here. If you show you know too much we start assigning bodies to you and put you to work," Dr. Abdullah said offering a sly smirk.

Lang turned for the door and felt the familiar vibration of his cell phone ringing. Drawing out the minute device, he answered the call and listened carefully to the irate caller. "James, I'm on my way, I'll be right there," Lang said as he snapped the phone back in his holster to race back to the scene.

CHAPTER EIGHTEEN

"Okay James, what's going on?" Lang asked, answering the second frantic incoming call.

"I told you that no good son of a bitch, Jeremy, had something to do with my cousin's murder. I went over to Charles' place and spoke with the neighbor who lives behind him. Do you know what he said? He told me this morning he found a black stereo speaker lying in his front yard right next to his big oak tree. And you know what else he found? He found a couple of arrows in the grass along the side of his house. So when I asked him if I could take a look see, he let me, and sure as shit, it was my cousin's stuff!"

"But how does that make Jeremy the killer?" Lang asked, trying to calm down the irate cousin.

"Well, that's when everything started getting interesting. I went across the street from where we found the stuff, spoke to them folks, and they said they found some stuff in their yard, too! They found a couple of arrows and some power tools. Turns out they were my cousin's, too. And get this—do you know who lives right behind them?"

"Who?" Lang asked.

"That asshole I told you about, Jeremy. The dumbass probably broke into my cousin's house to steal some shit and got caught. Then he left a trail of evidence straight from the back of my cousin's place right up to his garage. I'm telling you, I can see shit in his yard that belongs to my cousin."

"All right James, I'm sending Detective Gibson over to start collecting the stuff. I'm going to head back over to my office and start typing a search warrant for Jeremy's house."

Having tended to most of the conversation while scooting up the Interstate, Lang was in the homicide office within minutes. After he depressed the power switch, he fired up the outdated computer. With the tedious startup process just underway, Lang was certain this afforded him plenty of time to brew a fresh pot of Columbian roast coffee.

****

"Ma'am, I'm Detective Gibson from the Homicide Unit. I understand you found some items in your yard this morning." Gibson looked over his shoulder and felt comfortable no one, particularly the suspect, noticed his presence in the community.

"Yes, Detective. Please, come on in."

Gibson made his way through the simple but quaint abode. The formal living room was adorned with antique furniture handed down through the generations. The furnishings were, no doubt, heirlooms that had found their way from the motherland of Germany when they accompanied their owners who immigrated and settled in Highlandtown centuries ago. The ornately carved, dark-stained wood, decorated with beautifully embroidered tapestry seemed almost too beautiful to sit upon. Nonetheless, the lady insisted and Detective Gibson got right to work.

"Where are these items you found?"

"Well, when we saw them early this morning we brought them in; they're lying on the kitchen table. We knew the police were investigating something at Charles' house all day yesterday. He lives right behind us, you know. We were afraid a young child would get a hold of it and get hurt."

195

"Did you touch them with your bare hands?" Gibson asked with a wince.

"Yes, why we... oh my, I never thought to use gloves. Now my prints are all over the evidence."

"It's quite all right ma'am," the detective said reassuringly, "it happens all the time."

"Detective, what happened yesterday at Charles' house?"

"You haven't heard?"

"Not a thing." She sat patiently in her seat and rubbed her hands over her knees in suspense.

"Charles was found dead in his home yesterday. We're investigating his death."

"You mean Charles is dead! Was he murdered?" She cupped her hands over her mouth, hiding the shock that washed over her face.

"It appears that way, though the ME hasn't made an official ruling."

After he finished his interview, Gibson gathered the evidence from the kitchen table and discretely wrapped his overcoat around the items. He casually walked out to the Crown Victoria and placed the items in the back seat before driving back over to Charles' house. There he met the crime lab technician who was staged at the house. This was all done as a ploy to cause any suspects in the murder who may stumble through the neighborhood to believe that the police were still processing the original crime scene. Gibson pulled up in front of the location, nonchalantly removed the items from his car and transferred them into the side of the crime lab unit. The transaction went flawlessly, leaving the secret of the discovered evidence only with the detective and their finders.

****

"Your Honor, I apologize for disturbing your Sunday afternoon, but this is a matter that just can't wait." Lang stood in the center of the judge's living room and fished out

196

the application for the search warrant from his leather folder. "Detective, you work in the homicide unit; I certainly understand. It's not like you're wasting my time for a search warrant you're going to serve sometime next week. Please, have a seat while I read your application," the judge said, smiling as she stretched out her hand and took the application.

The Honorable Judge Alexia Rollins reclined in her easy chair wearing her favorite University of Maryland sweat suit and black poufy slippers as she flung her legs over one sidearm, nestling into one of her favorite relaxing positions. Lang sat patiently listening to an unseen hallway clock ticking away the seconds of the day as the judge vigilantly read through the narrative of events.

"What an asshole!" she suddenly blurted out ending all stillness. "He probably caved in this guy's skull so he could steal his shit to support his heroin addiction," she said with great confidence. "Detective, please raise your right hand. Do you solemnly swear and affirm under the penalties of perjury that the statements made here in this application and affidavit are true?"

"You know I do judge, or I wouldn't have brought it—"

The darting look over the papers edge indicated to the witty detective that the judge was looking for a more formal answer.

"Yes, your Honor, I do," Lang conceded.

"Very well, then," she said, suppressing her laughter behind her pursed lips. Turning to the appropriate page, Judge Rollins affixed her signature and authorized the search warrant for Jeremy's residence.

"Now, do me a favor," she said, as Lang prepared to slip out the door.

"And what's that, your Honor?" Lang asked.

"Be careful! I don't like seeing any of my officers getting hurt."

****

It was unanimously decided, without any consultation, the search warrant should be executed under the cover of evening's darkness. Secrecy was of the utmost importance even though James would call the detectives every hour for an update on the status of his cousin's investigation.

"James, we're running records," Lang offered, consoling the need to know.

Maintaining the integrity of the investigation at this tender juncture was of the utmost importance. Through an audit already carried out by a number of members of the family, several long guns and rifles were determined missing, and the day's efforts in locating them at local area pawn shops proved fruitless. Investigators were facing a killer who may be potentially armed with a high powered rifle equipped with a scope. Darkness would prove to be an ally that would render the scopes ineffective and hopefully allow the investigators to converge on the new lead without being placed in harm's way.

"We'll make our approach at 2200 hours," Lang explained to the warrant taskforce officers assembled late Sunday evening. "I need three guys out front covering the front door, and the rest of the team at the back door. Smitty and Jones, you guys need to cover the garage while we make entry. Any questions?"

The assembly of officers sat momentarily to see if any had questions. None did. All were aware of the task that lay before them and were eager to oblige the grieving family with the resolution that they so desperately wanted. Each officer made his way from the conference table into the precinct's parking lot where they would extract the needed equipment from the trunks of their cars. Bulletproof vests were slung overhead, then tightly strapped as officers weighed the potential danger they may face with the high powered rifle in a murderer's hands. Thigh holsters and gun belts were buckled into place as weapons checks were completed to ensure every officer's sidearm was properly

198

loaded; safeties were off, and ready to disperse a volley of lead fury for anyone intending to cause them harm and to thwart any opportunity for a desperate suspect to offer a counterattack. The stealthy, sleek, high intensity flashlights were tested to ensure no darkened corner would be left dimly lit.

With their equipment in place, the team mounted up in their nondescript sedans and assembled the parade of violence out to the main thoroughfare. Located only a short distance from the precinct, the motorcade zigzagged through the stilled neighborhoods where many families were assembled around the evening's news broadcasts of other murderous mayhem that had happened throughout the city over this violent weekend. After they found their target's street, headlights were extinguished as the motorcade made its final approach and slipped off to the curb's side under the darkness of the night. Quieted thuds could be heard up and down the street as the assault team exited their vehicles, closing their doors as softly as possible before quickly shuffling up the sidewalk and turning towards the intended residence.

As the three officers took up their assignments at the front of the house, the remainder formed into a single file line and wound their way towards the front porch using the dark swaying shadows for concealment. Without any formal command, muffled clicks could be heard as the team unsnapped their holsters and extracted their firearms from their resting positions. Smitty and Jones broke off, taking positions on opposing corners of the garage as directed; the remainder of them lined up along side of the house and geared up for their dynamic entry through the back door.

As the officers prepared to force the door open, it suddenly burst open without any warning, and a large male figure appeared in the doorway, straining his eyes to make out the silhouetted shadows in his backyard.

"Who the hell is out there? Get off my—"

Griffin leaped from his place of concealment, reached

up, grabbed the male figure by the back of his neck and tossed him over the concrete stairs onto the macadam driveway.

"Police! Search warrant! Get on the ground!" he yelled as he now pressed the muzzle of his .40 caliber Sig Sauer into the back of the man's head. "One stupid move and you're dead!"

The thunderous orders suddenly rang out from the remainder of the team members who were darting up the stairway and into the dwelling. As the shouts continued to resonate from deep within the abode, streams of lights could be seen frantically lasering in all directions through the draped windows.

"Hands in the air! Get on the ground! Get on the ground!" came the orders from an officer upon entering the front corner bedroom.

The pale white teen, clad in only a pair of faded jeans, immediately raised his hands and fell to his knees. He wept like a small child.

"I knew you were coming for me. I knew it," he cried uncontrollably.

"Face down on the ground," the officer ordered, as he flung the suspect face first, wrenching both wrists behind his back for cuffing.

In a matter of ninety seconds, the entire residence was secured, all of the occupants handcuffed and identified, and the search warrant initiated.

Lang walked in the wake of the aftermath after a task force officer notified him Jeremy was located in the front corner bedroom, crying since his arrest and wanting to speak to police about what had happened. In his long dark wool coat, Lang slipped around the corner and saw the young teen sitting on the floor, uncontrollably weeping.

"Are you Jeremy?" Lang asked.

"Yes sir, I am. I knew you guys were looking for me. It was only a matter of time. None of it was my fault, I'll tell you guys everything you want to know," he said through his wrenched face and streaming tears.

"Get him out to my car. I'll be out in a minute," Lang ordered.

Two officers yanked the suspect to his feet, grabbed a pair of tennis shoes and a hooded sweatshirt; they threw the items on the suspect to get him to headquarters as quickly as possible.

"What's going on here?" demanded the fatherly figure who was facedown at the foot of his back porch steps, one officer kneeling with a knee in his back.

"What's going on here is that it looks like your boy has been out burglarizing the neighborhood. We've got a search warrant. The problem is, in his last burglary, your son decided to beat the homeowner to death," the official said sharply.

****

Jeremy shuffled his chain linked feet across the dingy gray carpeted floor. His head hung down to his chest and tears trickled from the edge of his cheeks as he walked through the threshold of the second interview room and found his way to the prisoner's seat in the corner of the room. After they uncuffed their prisoner and saw the remorse already setting in, the detectives wasted no time and went right to work.

"Jeremy, I'm Detective Lang and this is Detective Gibson, we work with the Criminal Investigation Division here with the police department. As you may be aware, we are working an investigation where you have become a suspect. This is why you have now been arrested."

Jeremy looked up through his tears and nodded his head. "Mr. Charles' house," he acknowledged.

"Yes, Mr. Charles' house. We'd like to talk to you about what happened at Mr. Charles'—"

"I'll tell you everything you want to know. But I need to know something first—is Mr. Charles all right?"

The question completely stunned the two detectives who found themselves looking at each other in complete disbelief. Returning their gaze back onto their oblivious captive, Lang cleared his throat and informed Jeremy of Charles' fate.

"Um, Jeremy—Charles is dead—we're homicide detectives."

At first, the information almost seemed surreal. It was as if this whole thing was one big prank, orchestrated by one of his friends. He sat back and chuckled, waiting for the detectives to let him off the hook. But as Jeremy measured the somber countenance scripted across the two detective's faces, his eyes widened, giving Lang and Gibson every indication that their prisoner was now coming to the realization of his circumstances.

"Jeremy, we need to know everything that happened to Charles before he died."

Overwhelming shock completely engulfed Jeremy as he let out a scream followed by a fresh stream of tears.

"He's dead? Oh, my God, no! It can't be! Please tell me he isn't dead! Please!" Jeremy ranted as he stomped his sole against the floor. Then, just as quickly as he had flared up, Jeremy found a complete peace and calmness that allowed him to look up with a stone cold face and reiterate his offer to tell the detective's everything they needed to know.

"The whole thing was his idea," Jeremy confided. Lang and Gibson caught eyes once again as Jeremy started to spill the beans about his involvement in the botched burglary. "Mark and I used to do some odd jobs for Mr. Charles. We were over at his house last week when Mark saw something he wanted; I think it was a generator or something, and he decided we'd come back and get it Friday night while Mr. Charles was at the tavern. He always goes to the tavern on Friday nights. So we went to his house about 11:00. We didn't see his truck parked out front, so we knew he wasn't there. We went in the house, took some stuff and left. But Mark wanted more. What he got wasn't enough, so we ended up going back to the house and this time Mr. Charles' truck was parked out front.

"We carried the first haul out the back patio door. That's the way we snuck back in for the next load. But when we got inside, we saw the bedroom light on and thought Mr. Charles was up. That's when Mark walked over towards the hallway and motioned for me to come over. When I got over there, we peeked around the corner and saw Mr. Charles asleep in his bed. Mark wanted to make sure that Mr. Charles didn't wake up and catch us in his house. So he walked into the bedroom and found a big metal flashlight sitting on the bureau. Mark grabbed it, went over to the, and then gave him a good solid hit on the side of his head. That's when Mr. Charles woke up all pissed off.

"'You sons-of-bitches' he yelled at us. 'Get out of my house,'" Jeremy shuttered, the fresh memories of the violent torrent enveloping him. "That's when Mark went crazy. I've never seen anybody that mad! He went berserk, standing over Mr. Charles in his bed, swinging that flashlight like it was a baseball bat. Over and over he kept hitting him in the head, blood slinging everywhere. I couldn't stand to watch, so I turned, ran out the back door and threw up in the backyard."

"How long was it after you ran outside to throw up before Mark came out ?" Lang asked.

"It had to be several minutes, 'cause when he got to the back door he had an arm full of shit he was ready to carry back to his house."

"So where's this metal flashlight?"

"Mark took it with him and threw it in a yard dumpster at a neighbor's house just down the street from my house. That's where his bloody shirt is, too!"

"Jeremy, this is a really important question, and I need you to be completely honest with me. When we send officers over and recover that flashlight, are we going to find any of your bloody fingerprints on it?"

Jeremy sat and contemplated his answer. The detective's could see he was clearly taking his time to think through the question that simply required a 'yes' or 'no' for an answer. Jeremy drew in a deep breath, and with an exasperated exhale, "Yes," he said with some reservation, "Mark made me hit him a couple of times."

"I see. So tell me, Jeremy, what kind of stuff did Mark take from Mr. Charles' house?" Lang asked.

"Well, there was the generator I told you about, some fishing poles, power tools, and, oh yeah, the bolt action rifle."

Leaving their prisoner alone to wallow in his self pity, Lang and Gibson scooted into the squad room, jumped on their computer databases and researched the information provided. It was quickly confirmed that Jeremy and Mark both had juvenile records and were known as the local burglars for the neighborhood. Countless charges for fourth-degree burglary, drug possession charges, and a few disorderly conducts littered their records. But as the rap sheets spilled forth from the printer it became immediately apparent to both detectives that one of the two comrades was more of a leader, the other a follower.

"Hey Kenny, look at this," Gibson said, drawing his partner's attention to the host of aggravated assaults. "What do you think?"

"Looks like somebody may be suffering from a little amnesia."

****

As the darkness of night now shrouded the metropolitan area, Lang stepped into his sergeant's office. The sparkling skyline gave way through the cold crisp night that shined through the immense office glass window. Petrelli leaned forward, the stark light of his desk lamp catching the edge of his weary profile.

"So, what's the next step?" the sergeant asked.

"Jeremy gave it up, put himself there, but named Mark as the one who carried out the assault. But—"

"But what?"

"When we run the two records, Jeremy's is pretty violent and extensive. Mark's only has a few minor offenses. We're thinking that Jeremy probably carried out the assault. The problem is we still have this Mark guy hanging out there, and he supposedly has one of the rifles that belongs to the victim," Lang explained.

"So are you thinking we need to do another search warrant?" the sergeant asked in confirmation.

"Yes. In fact, we're thinking of getting a 'no knock' warrant and sending in the tactical unit. The rifle this kid has is a hunting rifle, and his bedroom is on the third floor of the apartment building—a great place for a sniper attack."

Petrelli leaned back in his chair and folded his hands. "I agree. I'll line up the tactical unit and tell them we want to make a pre-dawn entry."

"Perfect. I'll start busting out the application for the search warrant and wake up a judge."

CHAPTER NINETEEN

The night was exhausting. While Lang sat at his desk and orchestrated the chattering computer keys and composed the authoritative document that would permit the investigators entry into a potentially dangerous location, Gibson secured their prisoner and caught a few winks. Lang pressed on deep into the night, finished his composition and obtained approval from a bleary-eyed judge. Lang headed straight back to the office and arrived with the sealed search warrant. When he arrived he found a well-rested and eager group of former special ops soldiers prepared to thrust their way into the dangerous dwelling to apprehend the remaining homicide suspect.

As the two detectives prepared to enter the briefing room, Gibson tapped Lang on the shoulder and offered a respite.

"Why don't you sit in the back of the room, get some rest, and let me handle this. You're going to need to be rested for the interview with Mark when we get him." It was a refreshing offer, and Lang knew a quick power nap would provide him with enough strength to carry on throughout the early morning and into a lingering afternoon. And with that offer, Lang sat back and closed his eyes.

****

The fortress sat atop a local business and provided ample parking around the entire circumference of the building. Unfortunately, the description provided by the pre-raid surveillance indicated the parking lot was well-lit and wide open from every direction and offered no areas of cover or concealment that would aid in protecting the team's heavily armed assault on the house. As the team mounted their suburban van, last minute equipment and weapons checks were conducted to ensure all were in communication and appropriately armed if the unannounced intrusion became confrontational.

Lang and Gibson took their positions in their unmarked frigate just a block from the target location while still within eyesight. Their timing would be essential in helping secure the outer perimeter as the plan required Lang to sweep up next to the house and drop off Gibson, who would synch up a weak point in the perimeter next to the main thoroughfare. The last second deployment would ensure complete surprise.

The two detectives sat patiently in their Crown Victoria that purred on the roadside with its light doused. Gibson lifted his handheld radio, adjusted the volume knob, and stared at the square black box awaiting the command. Within seconds the order came and the band of blue brotherhood was propelled into motion.

The large dark van streaked by Lang and Gibson's position as Lang ripped the gear selector into drive and scooted in behind the speeding convoy. The panel van found the exterior side stairwell on the west end of the building and veered to a stop in front of the stairway; this provided some limited protection for the advancing troops.

The side door slid open as the tactical officers jumped from the opening's ledge much like paratroopers would jump into enemy territory. One by one the officers followed behind the other and tucked their weapons at a low-ready and formed their stick. They snaked their way around the front corner of the van, the team streamed straight for the front door as each member of the team targeted a specific window as they left their area of protection provided the bulky blue van provided.

In one fluid sensation, the ram sheared the main front door from its hinges and the team continued their race up the interior flight of steps. Another crashing sound followed by an explosion with an intensely brilliant flash of white light confirmed to the surveillance team that the tactical unit has entered the main floor of the residence.

****

The darkened Crown Victoria swerved into position just under the second story window and paused long enough for Gibson to jump out of the passenger's seat and take cover beneath the window. With his dark suit and long black overcoat draped over him, Gibson leaned back into the shadow of the wall and extracted his semi-automatic from its battered leather holster. After he gave a quick glance to the left and right, Gibson continued surveying his area of responsibility as the tactical officers repeatedly yelled "Police, search warrant," as their voices faded while they penetrated deeper into the building.

That's when Gibson heard a muffled tapping. The sound was deep, dull, and resounded in three rapid successions before it ended just nanoseconds after the three round burst and shards of glass rained down upon his head.

What the hell was that? He shifted his position out from beneath the shattering window and glanced skyward for any indication the cause.

****

Smitty was assigned as the number two man on the stick. Well-shielded by the bunker man who was always in the first position, Smitty knew the bunker man totally relied on him to address any confrontations the team would experience as they rounded the corner from atop the interior steps.

When the team turned left, they immediately found themselves in the master bedroom of the residence, the two home owners lying in bed. The SWAT Team's repetitious shouts announcing who they were and their intentions to carry out the court ordered search warrant startled the slumbering couple.

"Police! Don't move!" came the order from Smitty as he zeroed on the two with his sights. "Let me see your hands! Let me see your hands!" he said, nudging the muzzle tip of his M4 carbine assault rifle towards the couple.

The husband rolled from his side to his back and flung the covers off himself.

"Get the hell out of my house, you assholes! Get out!"

"Police Department! Get you hands in the air," Smitty commanded of the angered homeowner who was now on his feet by his bedside.

"I said get the hell out of my house," the home owner replied as he stepped backwards towards a bureau situated in the corner next to the bed.

"Hands up!" the tactical officer ordered again as he focused his front sight on the husbands torso. Smitty barley remembered seeing the rifle extracted from the rear of the bureau and leveled towards him before he depressed his trigger with a short even squeeze. The M4 operated smoothly and proficiently as the trigger mechanism activated, pushed the firing pin forward in three repetitive movements and sent the deadly rounds down range and struck the noncompliant aggressor as intended.

The three rounds perforated the man's chest and ripped the central vital organs the sternum protected. As the rounds tore through his back, they continued their flight through the glass window that was behind the assailant and instantly sent small clear fragments of debris down below.

"Shots fired," the voice rang out over the secured radio channel. "Start a medic! Suspect is down!" The officer's heavy breathing lingered for a fraction of a second before he let off of the transmission button of the communications device.

The short announcement and request started a flurry of activity as the officers secured the outer perimeter. They switched to a variety of communication devices as they made the necessary notifications. One detective flipped his radio channel back to the precinct channel and urgently broke through the routine calls of service; he requested police dispatch to start an ambulance and command staff to the location. Another ripped his Nextel cell phone from its holster and woke his sleeping upper echelon and made notification of the measure they had just exercised. Almost immediately the communications center liaison console lit up and informed him of the situation; this prompted his notification to the Operations Bureau Colonel and the Chief of Police.

The threat neutralized, the tactical medic jumped into action. The emergency responder pulled gauze and bandages from his waist side medical kit as he raced against the clock while blood spilled freely from the three distinct wounds.

Davis cleared the first floor of the house and formed up the remaining members while they pushed the stick towards the unchallenged stairwell. Jeffers, who was now manning the thirty-five-pound bunker, clicked on the front-mounted lights and scurried towards the base of the steps. As he peeked around the corner with his sidearm peering over the top of the shield, he was immediately startled by a barely clad male wandering down the steps.

"Freeze! Police!" he ordered. But the subject continued walking down the steps towards the team, ignoring the order. Davis assessed this assailant. *He's wearing a pair of boxer shorts. Check his hands—empty!* As the subject stepped just in range, Davis retracted his handgun from it lofty position and smashed the top edge of the bunker into the man's face.

You deserved that you no good son of a bitch! Davis watched the unconscious subject slump to the floor like a leaning sack of potatoes. He placed his handgun back over the edge of the bunker; Davis and his team trampled over the downed subject and continued their mission to clear the second floor. As his team returned to the upper landing of the stairway, Davis looked down to see that the last man on his stick had identified the subject, whose face he had just smashed, as the second suspect being sought in the murder. It was only seconds before he was handcuffed and whisked away to the awaiting detectives.

****

"Kenny," Gibson called from halfway across the parking lot.

The two converged near the front door entrance just as the tactical officers escorted Mark from the residence. His legs were shackled and hands cuffed behind his back; the officers had taken just enough time to drape a few clothes over their scrawny, pale captive.

"We'll have to talk later; not in front of him," Gibson explained as he wandered off to see one last task completed before he rode with Lang and the suspect back to headquarters.

The ride was quiet and somber as heat from the vents slowly chased away the chill that had settled into the detective's bones. He stoic faced stared blankly out the half-frosted window as Mark sat quietly in the back seat and wondered what about his future when this night ended.

****

With their prisoner secured in the interview room, Gibson cornered Lang in the squad area with the news.

"Jones told me the guy they shot in the house was our suspect's dad," Gibson said.

"Okay, and?" Lang asked.

"…and he's dead!"

"He's dead? What happened?" Lang inquired.

"The team made their entry and woke up the old man. He refused to comply with their orders and pulled a rifle out from behind the bureau. Smitty didn't have a choice! The old man leveled the rifle right at him!"

"So, we have to go in that room, get him to give us a full confession, and then tell him his father is dead?"

"Pretty much," Gibson confirmed.

Damn.

"He has to know. When they brought him out from upstairs they walked him right past the body didn't they?"

"Yeah, but he seemed to think his dad had some other medical problem., I don't think he's connected the shooting and his dad, yet."

"How do you hear gunshots, see your dad lying still in a pool of blood, and not know he isn't going to wake up again?" Lang asked.

"I don't know, but I'm guessing he ain't all that smart!"

"Well, let's go find out."

The two detectives gathered the necessary paperwork: pens, pads, and a Miranda warning form. As they casually walked into the interview room, Mark raised his head up from the sleeping position he had found on the tables edge. He immediately asked the one question the detectives hoped they could avoid until the end of the interview.

"How's my dad?"

Lang paused and thought carefully before he gave his answer. The experienced detective knew there was nothing he could do for the father who lay dead in his bedroom and waited for the other homicide squad to respond. The son, on the other hand, was in a huge legal quandary that, if not carefully sorted out, could cost him the remainder of his life even though the detectives didn't believe he was the primary aggressor in their murder investigation.

"Mark, I don't have any updates right now but we'll keep you posted about his condition." *That's a straight up lie.* "Right now, you're under arrest because of something that happened at Charles' house," Lang explained as Mark's head dropped in remorse. "Mark, I'm not going to sit here and play head games with you. We're not going to pull the 'good cop, bad cop' trick; we're not even going to sit here and make up shit to get you to tell us what happened. We will tell you we've arrested Jeremy and he's talked to us. The problem is he says the whole thing was your idea," Lang explained.

"That liar!" Mark screamed and exhaled his frustration. "It was all his idea!"

"I think I understand, but we need to advise you of your

rights and have you waive them if you want to talk to us about this incident." Lang slid the form across the desk, the ink pen lying on top waiting to be used to affix the required signature.

"No problem! I'll tell you everything you need to know."

Lang carefully went through the regimen of advising Mark's rights to him. After each of the five enumerated points were read aloud to him, Mark indicated he understood his rights and offered no questions. As the two worked their way through the legal form, Lang read aloud the waiver clause to which Mark again expressed his understanding and willingness to speak with the police about the incident. As Lang concluded, Mark lifted the pen with no hesitation and signed his name, indicating his election to waive his rights. As he laid the pen back down onto the tabletop Mark asked a surprising question.

"So, how's Mr. Charles doing?"

Are both of these guys oblivious? Jackasses!

Lang and Gibson both sat stunned at the question. They had just successfully secured a waiver of rights from the young man who was unknowingly facing murder charges and still needed to be advised that his father had died. The egg-shells the two detectives walked on had just become a little more brittle.

"Mark, that's what makes what you say today so important, Mr. Charles is dead. He didn't survive the beating." Lang paused, and took in the suspect's stunned countenance.

Mark's face flushed pale as he slung himself backwards in his seat in utter and complete disbelief.

"Dead! He's dead? That means—I can be charged with murder?" he asked.

"Yes, Mark, that's right, that's why what you tell us today is so very important," Lang explained.

"Because Jeremy is saying that this was all my idea," Mark reasoned. "No! No! I'm not going down for this bullshit—it was all his doing! He was the one who knew Mr. Charles and he was the one who wanted to break into his house," Mark explained.

"Well Mark, that's what we're here to figure out. We need

to find out the truth."

As he collected his senses and finished wiping the bloody mess from his nose administered by the incapacitated swat of the bunker, Mark gathered himself and poured out the sequence of events that brought him to the cramped little interview room. He described for the investigators how Jeremy had done some yard work for Mr. Charles on a few occasions and how he had recently been in his house and saw all of his hunting rifles. Knowing the pretty penny he could get for them and some other items he eyed up, Mark recalled the day when Jeremy approached him about burglarizing the retiree's residence.

"'Look. Every Friday night he goes down to the tavern. He ain't got no wife, no kids, so the house should be empty,' he told me. And like an idiot, I listened," Mark said.

He continued with his recollection of the night when they went to Charles' house. Much like a seaman recalling a long-lost adventure, Mark delved into the details that the detectives needed to hear. He explained how earlier in the evening they had gone to the house, stole some items, and took it back to Jeremy's house. When they returned shortly after midnight for another haul, they were stunned when they noticed Charles' truck sitting out front.

"'Come on! Let's go in,' he told me. I didn't want to go in, but I did. We found him sleeping in bed. He was snoring pretty loud, but Jeremy wanted to make sure he was out cold, so he found a MAG flashlight sitting up on the bedroom dresser, grabbed it, and—" Mark couldn't find the words. His breath abated him.

"And what?" Lang asked encouraging Mark to continue with the story. But the memory of the violent attack caused him to convulse and twitch as he grew sick at the very memory of that dark night.

Tears welled up in his eyes. "That's when Jeremy started beating him in the head. Over and over, he wouldn't stop. The thudding noise it made every time he hit Mr. Charles' head almost made me throw up. That's when I ran outside."

Mark left no detail unanswered as he answered every

question the detectives posed to him that surrounded that Friday night. His ability to recall every instance of the events surpassed that of his co-defendant's and the detectives felt their hunch was correct in thinking that Jeremy was the primary actor in this vicious murder. Unfortunately, with only three people present at the time of the assault, one dead and two pointing the finger at each other, the detectives would need something more substantial to prove beyond a reasonable doubt who played what role. In the meantime there was one last matter that needed to be contended with.

"Mark, tonight you're being charged with first degree murder. We'll need to type up your charging document, take you downstairs, fingerprint and photograph you and then we'll get you over to the court commissioner's office for your bail hearing. With the seriousness of this charge, the commissioner typically denies issuing a bail and you'll be housed at the county jail until trial," Lang explained.

Mark slumped over, his head hung in shame as the realization of the moment seeped into his mind.

"And what about my father?" he asked as one last matter of business.

Lang sat forward and slid a little closer to Mark. Placing his hand upon his shoulder, he faced the inevitable news.

"Mark, because Jeremy said you stole those guns from Mr. Charles' house, we wrote what is called a 'no-knock search warrant.' That lets our officers enter a house without first knocking and saying who we are. It lets us use the element of surprise so we stay safe. When the SWAT Team went into your house they found your parents in the bedroom. They told them who they were and why they were there, but your dad kept yelling at them to 'get out of my house.' When they didn't, your dad reached for a rifle he had near his bedside—"

"I know which one you're talking about," Mark added.

"Mark, he aimed that rifle at our officers... your dad was shot. And even though there was an ambulance nearby for such a situation, he didn't make it Mark. Your dad died."

****

215

She stood as erect as possible against the dark wood stained table as tears streamed down her face and dripped onto its edge. Doris Riley shook nervously as the judge took his seat at the bench and called her case as a formality.

"Your Honor, the state and defense have entered into a binding plea agreement I believe satisfies both the state's and defense's needs," the State's Attorney announced.

"Very well," answered the judge, elated the case wouldn't be drawn out through a long and arduous trial. "And how will we be proceeding today counsel?"

"Your Honor," piped up the defense counsel, "we'll be proceeding with a guilty plea with the understanding the state will not recommend a sentence any longer than ten years in the Department of Correction and my client will be subjected to an appropriate psychological treatment program as deemed by the court."

"All right, I'll hear the statement of facts to see if the facts support the guilty plea." The judge adjusted his robe and leaned back in his leather chair and waited to hear the facts of the case.

Mrs. Williams opened the manila folder and read aloud the events that encompassed Stevie's last days prior to his death.

At the mere mention of his name the mother wept bitterly as she longed to take back that moment in her life. She wished to live as most mothers: loving, holding, and nurturing their children. As fleeting as the minutes were, so too was life. Both of her children were now dead, and she agreed to a plea offer of ten years, a handsome sentence in some jurisdictions for the accidental death of a child caused by the rituals of daily abuse.

Mrs. Williams read the facts with a plain monotone voice, removed the true emotions that both the family and detectives held inside of them. Everyone who gathered in the courtroom--the judge, attorneys, families, strangers, officers, and detectives-- sat in complete amazement as the facts of a cold-hearted mother were uttered in the legal chamber and resonated off the dark stained walls. Many sat and shook their heads as they tried to contemplate how anyone could have generated such animosity and disdain for a helpless child. They wondered how anyone could have repeatedly tossed this helpless child down the cellar steps like an old worn out broken toy. Before long, every eye in the courtroom was glared the accused, and she felt the weight of their stare as it ripped straight through her. Doris' blood drained from every corner of her body as the room grew close and cold. Judgment was about to be passed.

"Ms Riley," the judge snapped, "I find that the probable cause is sufficient to find you guilty and hereby sentence you to ten consecutive years in the Department of Correction for the State of Maryland. Court is adjourned." The judge pounded the gavel on his bench, sprung up from his chair, and marched out of the courtroom in utter disgust.

"Is that all we could get?" Lang asked as he leaned over towards Winthrop.

"I'm afraid so. We could only charge her with the manslaughter charge."

"And what about the other case where the infant died?"

"We looked at it downtown at the ME's office, but we didn't find anything substantive that would permit us to get a court order to exhume the body."

"So she gets away with murder?" Lang asked.

"It is what it is," answered Winthrop shrugging his shoulders.

****

Lang straggled into the squad room and plopped himself down into the gray plush office chair positioned at his desk. Glancing over to his phone, he recognized the familiar indicator that a voicemail message had been left; undoubtedly, a family member calling for an update on the most recent murder investigation. Taking a quick look at the clock, Lang considered the remaining time in his shift and decided to see who was inquiring of his services. As he wedged the receiver between his ear and shoulder, he quickly ran through the automated menus, punched in his access code, and waited for the message.

"Detective Lang? It's Jeremy over here at the county jail. There's something I need to tell you, something I need to get off my chest."

CHAPTER TWENTY

"Your Honor, calling off of the docket, State versus Jeremy Cullum," said the Assistant States Attorney, Mrs. Andrea Reynolds.

"Sheriff, would you please bring in Jeremy Cullum from the lockup," said the judge.

Under the escort of three deputies who flanked all sides, Jeremy lumbered into the courtroom, his hair unkempt and uncombed; he appeared completely drained and fatigued. As he took his position behind the defense table, he glanced back into the galley and waved to his mother who sat and dabbed tears from her cheeks.

Given the magnitude of the charges and the weight of the potential sentence hanging over his head, Jeremy realized that his fate was inevitable. He faced forward and stared blankly against the Great Seal of Maryland that hung above the bench on the back wall.

Charles' family, who showed up in full force, filled much of the galley on the one side of the courtroom while Jeremy's mother, father, and a few straggling friends occupied only the front bench on the other side of the galley.

"Mr. Simmons, how does your client intend to plea today?" asked the judge.

"Guilty, Your Honor," he replied.

"Mrs. Reynolds, do you have a statement of probable cause prepared to read to the court in support of this guilty plea?" the judge asked.

"I do your Honor. If it would please the court, on or about the date of…"

As the horrific violence unfolded in narrative form, Charles' family drew closer together. Some allowed their tears of mourning to be seen, others embraced for comfort to endure the required legal ordeal. While the tragedy of losing Charles at the hands of a young man who had only been eighteen years of age was difficult to handle, the family was thankful Jeremy had finally confided to the detectives he was the sole person who had beaten Charles, and Mark was only there to help facilitate the planned burglary.

Every eye was fixated on the attractive Andrea Reynolds who continued to read aloud the events that culminated in the investigative effort that brought Jeremy Cullum before the court with such heavy charges. Jeremy continued staring blankly as the details were spelled out to everyone's horror; the two boys entering the house with the intention of burglarizing it and the repeated blows to the back of Charles' head. But, most astonishing to the audience was how investigators later learned from Jeremy that following the vicious assault and burglary, he had returned to the scene alone, without his partner in crime and moved the body from the bedroom to the bathroom in some valiant attempt to render aid to his dying victim.

After rendering some forty blows to the top of the head, Jeremy stole the items of choice and left the victim for dead. But about an hour after he left the house, Jeremy described how he had returned to the scene to check on Mr. Charles. He found him unconscious in bed where he had severely beaten him and decided if he could get him to the bathroom and clean him up he would probably be all right. After he removed the victim's clothing, he slung the limp body over his shoulders and worked his way to the bathroom and braced his hands against the walls for support. The wrist watch had become damaged when Charles attempted to defend himself. When it was bumped against the bathroom doorway, the backing came free and the battery dislodged, forever memorializing the time the body was transferred from the bedroom to the bathroom. Unable to maintain his victim's weight at the bathroom sink, he sat his victim on the toilet while he retrieved a towel from the linen closet and wiped away the coagulating blood. When the towel proved useless, the only alternative that seemed reasonable to the frantic suspect was to flip the victim over the tub's edge and try to wash him clean. But as the blood poured out from the devastating wound and into the bathtub drain, Jeremy realized that his efforts were pointless, and his victim was dead.

"Your Honor. That concludes the state's case."

A hush fell over the courtroom as every eye looked upon the judge who sat quietly at the bench, his glasses pinched between his fingers, the frame caught between his teeth, as he was lost in thought. In a calculated movement, the judge leaned forward and stared at the charged offender until both made eye contact with one another.

"The court finds there is sufficient probable cause to support the guilty plea, and I do hereby find you guilty of first degree murder," scolded the judge.

A sigh of relief escaped from each of Charles' family members and could be heard throughout the room. Now the suspense rose as the court would hear arguments in litigation from the defense attorney as to why Jeremy Cullum should receive a lighter penalty than the state desired. The defense counsel painted Jeremy as a lost child who never really experienced a true childhood and therefore was another victim of a failing society. As Jeremy's counsel rambled from one stage of his life to the next, the judge sat patiently with his eyebrow raised and waited for the defense counsel to rest on his arguments. And when he had said all that he could have, the defense rested and the judge passed judgment without haste.

"Mr. Cullum, in the tenure this court has experienced, and with all of the violent crimes that have been presented here, this is probably the most violent and senseless offense this court has ever witnessed. You entered the house of a retiree, someone who had worked hard all his life, who was already overcome by his inebriated state, and you mercilessly overtook him with such hatred and violence that the medical examiner stopped counting the blows you inflicted!" The judge rocked in his chair, cupped his hands, and looked away as he tried to purge his mind of the imagery of the crime scene created during the reading of the statement of facts. A determined look replaced his countenance. The judge slung forward in his chair and glared at the defendant. "Never have I seen such violence," his voice said with adamant strength. "It goes without saying I am compelled to measure reasonableness regarding a punishment as well as the probability of rehabilitation. And as I survey the evidence in this case, I must say the anger you purported on this helpless, intoxicated man gives me clear indication you lack the ability to be rehabilitated. Furthermore, I am also compelled to weigh the safety of the community in determining an appropriate sentence. Therefore, it is hereby ordered you shall spend the rest of your natural given life in the Department of Correction for the State of Maryland. Mr. Cullum, to be perfectly clear, I see no other just punishment."

As quickly as the words fell off the judges' lips, the family in the galley erupted with such euphoria and joy that the judge grabbed his gavel and beat it repeatedly against the bench.

"Order! Order! Order in my courtroom!" he yelled, rising from the bench.

As quickly as they had erupted, the family called themselves into check. The judge, who was completely unsettled by the event then addressed the family.

"It does not give me joy to sentence a man to jail for the remainder of his natural life. While I sympathize with you and your family for your loss, we need to remember the loss to society is not one but two losses: the loss of the victim when he so violently died and the loss of an eighteen year old boy, another member of our society, who made a bad decision and will never be a productive member of our society. So while your grief is beginning to subside, another family is just beginning to experience their loss."

****

Sitting poised with her long slender legs crossed behind her oak desk, Andrea Reynolds perused the file one last time as Lang stepped into her doorway.

"Are we ready?" Lang asked as he captured her attention.

"I think so. We'll be before Judge Prichard today."

"And what motions did they file?" Lang asked.

"The usual—motions to suppress the statement, suppress the evidence, you know. Look, you've been through this routine a hundred times; it's a piece of cake!"

They gathered the conglomeration of folders and legal books and Lang and Reynolds then made their way into courtroom number four, the formal trial courtroom reserved for the hearing. They organized the files quickly as the deputy stepped from the back paneled door and announced the entrance of the judge.

"All rise for the Honorable Anthony Prichard."

"Please be seated," the judge countered with a small motion of his hand while he sat down.

Lang's recollection of events that had transpired a few months prior now surfaced and his concern suddenly grew deep. The article splashed in all of the local news papers which drew a black mark against the bench. Judge Prichard's arrest for his lack of reasoning concerning the driving abilities of intoxicated persons brought him under a great deal of scrutiny by both the public and his peers. Nonetheless, he took the bench with great dignity in spite of his adversity.

This motions hearing became necessary because of the defense's attempts to remove much of the evidence that had been stacked against his client. Therefore, the onus was laid upon him to initiate the proceedings, quickly address each issue and not lose the court's interest.

Opening remarks by both sides went splendidly. Logical, methodical, and mind provoking, Al Snyder presented a brilliant presentation concerning the legality of the confession his client offered.

"Your Honor, I would not suggest the police didn't do an adequate job of administering my client's Miranda rights to him nor would I suggest they failed to meet the minimum legal requirements in securing a waiver from my client. I would propose to the court, however, that my client's mental capacity renders him incapable of understanding his rights even though he indicated to the detectives he did understand his rights," Snyder argued.

"Then call your first witness Mr. Snyder," ordered the judge.

"Your Honor, the defense would like to call Mrs. Patricia Stevens to the stand."

Patricia Stevens was a court appointed psychologist who had been afforded ample time to assess Mark, his ability to understand his legal rights and to determine if he was even capable of understanding such terms. After qualifying her as an expert witness in the field of psychology, Mr. Snyder carefully questioned Mrs. Stevens about her assessment. She methodically revealed to the court how she measured Mark's IQ which was determined to be a mere 63. Satisfied with that portion of the testimony, Mr. Snyder focused Mrs. Stevens' attention on the traumatic events that unfolded just hours prior to the time police offered Mark the opportunity to waive his rights. But when the defense's witness offered testimony that indicated Mark's knowledge of the death of his father had a significant impact on his ability to reason his rights, the judge became indignant.

"Mrs. Stevens are you suggesting that Mark was incapable of making a rational decision pertaining to his rights because of his father's death?" the judge asked with great irritation.

"Yes, I am."

The judge leaned forward against the bench. "Mrs. Stevens! Mr. Snyder already provided the court with the videotaped confession. And in reviewing that videotape, it is painfully clear Mark was not told about his father's death until *after* he made a full and complete confession! Explain to me how you are able to come to such a finding!"

The oversight proved quite embarrassing for both the psychologist and the defense counsel. And in spite of his efforts to suggest to the court Mark had somehow assumed his father was dead from passing his body during his arrest, the judge wasn't buying the argument.

Mr. Snyder quickly finished with his current witness and called the next. "Your Honor, I would like to call Reverend Samuel Faulkner to the stand next."

With his tattered and worn Bible clinched under his left arm, the Priest took the stand and raised his right hand and received the administration of the oath.

"Do you solemnly swear and affirm under the penalties of perjury that the testimony that you are about to give is the truth, whole truth, and nothing but the truth?" the clerk asked.

"I do."

Father Samuel Faulkner took his seat and rested the Holy Scriptures on the ledge before him where the microphone was mounted. Mr. Snyder posed his first question, which sought an explanation from the priest about how he had met Mark. Father Faulkner leaned in towards the microphone to begin this recollection.

"I was doing a jail visitation," he jerked back from the microphone as his first words boomed through the overhead speakers. "...as I do each week at the detention center, when I met Mark, who was a new inmate in one of the pods to which I am assigned. He was seated at a table in the common area when I approached him. He appeared despondent."

Lang leaned over to Gibson in the galley and whispered "I'd be despondent, too, if I were charged with murder, and my dad was killed during my arrest."

The priest continued, "So I sat down next to him and asked him if I could read him some scripture. He didn't respond, so I sat down anyway and read Psalm 23 to him. After I read it to him, I asked him 'What did you think about that scripture?' but he didn't respond. So then I asked him if he understood the scripture and he simply shook his head that he didn't, so I explained it to him."

"Father, in the last six months that you've been in contact

225

with Mark during these jail visitations, have you had the opportunity to read other passages of scripture to him that he did not understand?"

"I did."

Lang glanced up at the judge and noticed the blank stare written across his face as his hand clenched his rosary and rubbed the crucifix between his fingers. The judge leaned back into a more relaxed position and stared up at the ceiling as the defense's arguments came to a close. It was now time for the court to render a decision in the matter. The judge sat quietly with his eyes closed as he bounced his fingertips off one another with the rosary still threaded between his fingers and dangling in front of him.

"Now, regarding the defendant's confession. I must say that the detectives performed admirably in light of the heavy circumstances in front of them. Never have I seen such professionalism extended in such a case. However, I must say that while I do not regard the testimony from Mrs. Stevens with a great weight, I do hold Father Faulkner's testimony in high esteem. What was most compelling is his account of the reading of Psalm 23, a rather simplistic verse from the Bible. Nonetheless, it is my opinion that someone incapable of understanding the 23rd Psalm is also incapable of understanding their Constitutional rights. Therefore, it is my ruling that the defendant's confession be inadmissible during the course of his criminal trial."

****

The cool, crisp October morning bit with a chill as the morning's sun rose and highlighted the fire red and brilliant orange leaves that were preparing to set themselves loose and blanket the ground. The courtroom filled with the anticipated family and friends who would represent both sides of this murder. Detective Lang greeted Andrea Reynolds who was already prepared and seated at the trial table.

"Are you sure we can win this without the confession?" Lang asked.

"I'm pretty sure we can. And if we don't get everything, so what? We already have the actual killer behind bars for life. Look, with the witnesses seeing him near the house that night, the stolen stuff in his house, and the blood drops that DNA shows belong to Charles on the pair of pants in his bedroom, I feel very certain we can show a jury his involvement in this murder," she said.

As the court was called to order, Judge Prichard entered the courtroom, a steaming hot mug of coffee in one hand and his rosary and Bible in the other. He briskly climbed the steps, sat down in his high back, leather bound chair and initiated the proceedings.

As the jury pool marched into the courtroom, the candidates list was expediently whittled down to the required twelve jurors and two alternates; seven women and five men. Andrea Reynolds felt confident with the selection. With the foreman named and given his instructions, the stage was set for opening arguments.

With extreme confidence, Andrea Reynolds marched across the courtroom floor and took a position immediately in front of the jury box. With her wrists clasped behind her back, she smiled and greeted the jurors.

"Ladies and gentlemen of the jury, good morning. Today when you woke up, I would venture to say many of you were dreading having to report for jury duty." The jurors smiled at the humor. "You hoped somehow you would be able to manage to slip through the cracks, be released from your duty and return to your normal everyday life. But, here you sit, and for good reason, because today is a very important day. It's an important day for a defendant who will be asking you to weigh the evidence of the charges of murder that are facing him. It is also an important day for a family who asks you to weigh that very same evidence and find justice for a loving son and father who are no longer with them.

"Today is a very important day because you will begin hearing testimony about how two boys entered the residence of Charles Nelson and burglarized his house. You'll hear about how they returned, found Mr. Nelson home alone in bed fast

227

asleep they caved in his skull with a MAG flashlight. You'll also hear about how, while Mr. Nelson lay dying in his bedroom, the two boys gathered up more property and made off with hundreds of dollars in property.

"As many of you know, evidence is a very crucial part of any successful case, and I am here to tell you we have lots of evidence. As I present the witnesses to the court and to you, listen carefully to what each has to say: the family member who found Charles dead in his house; the responding officers who secured the scene; the medical examiner who will describe to you they stopped counting the impact injuries after finding at least twenty distinctive blows; and the detectives who literally found the trail of evidence that led them to the first suspect and the trail of evidence that lead them to the second suspect, Markus Adams.

"As you can see, ladies and gentlemen, today is a very important day!"

The legal metronome clicked away in perfect rhythm. Andrea Reynolds called her first witness, James, who had found his cousin. Following his heart-wrenching account of his ghastly discovery, the first responding officers took the stand describing the crime scene in its entirety. Next, in logical order, came the crime lab technician who had meticulously documented, labeled and collected every piece of evidence. Photographs of the scene, including the grizzly aftermath, appeared on a screen situated across the courtroom. Everyone viewing the pictures gasped in horror at the pictures that so vividly revealed the true brutality of Charles' death. Finally, the detectives took the stand and described the trail of evidence that led to the suspect's home and the bloody pair of jeans they found in Mark's attic bedroom. The State covered everything in its presentation. Everything, that is, except Mark's confession.

And in good defensive form, Mr. Snyder quickly pointed to the fact that, yes, his client had stolen items, but the police didn't have enough evidence to say his client committed murder. One by one, Mr. Snyder introduced his witnesses to the jurors; they were mostly character witnesses who portrayed

Mark as someone who got caught up in the wrong crowd and followed the wrong people. As the defense finally rested its side, the two attorneys had one last shot at convincing the jury in their closing arguments. All said and done, the jurors were dismissed to their deliberation room. This is they would remain for the next five hours finally decide the fate of Markus Adams.

****

"Has the jury reached a verdict?" asked the court reporter after their return to the jury box.

"We have."

"What say you to count one, murder in the first degree?"

"Not guilty."

"What say you to count two, assault in the first degree?"

"Not guilty."

"What say you to count three, assault in the second degree?"

"Not guilty."

"What say you to count four, burglary in the fourth degree?"

"Guilty."

Infuriated, Honorable Judge Anthony Prichard leaned forward, his face beet red as he slung his rosary across his tabletop in utter frustration. The judge finished the proceeding, dismissed everyone from the courtroom but ordered t the jurors to remain seated in the juror box. When the courtroom was cleared, the judge unleashed his wrath.

"I have never seen in my entire career such a reckless miscarriage of justice!" he yelled. "How on earth you reached a decision of 'not guilty' on the charge of first degree murder is beyond me! The State presented sufficient evidence to show the defendant was present during the murder and did nothing to stop the vicious assault. Furthermore, he did nothing to aid the helpless dying victim. He could have called 911 or rendered some sort of aid himself, but instead, he gathered up in his arms property that did not rightfully belong to him and made his escape. And there was the victim's blood that was found on the bottom portion of his pants. Most importantly, you should know that subsequent to his arrest, the defendant made a confession to police." The jurors all sat in stunned amazement at the revelation. *Why wasn't his confession presented during the course of the trial?*

"But you, in your ignorance and pity for a defendant whose father was killed by the police during the course of his arrest, couldn't find the common sense to render a guilty finding. You should be ashamed of yourselves for such a miscarriage of justice. My prayer is that your decision to let a murderer walk away from these charges will haunt you the rest of your days—you're dismissed!"

****

Cloaked in a vibrant red jumpsuit with "DOC INMATE" freshly painted in white across his back, Jeremy shuffled down the long, wide, gray hallway in his shackles and used all his strength to keep his orange plastic sandals from slipping off of his stocking feet. Escorted by a guard, Jeremy carried his blanket and mat as he followed the trail of fluorescent lights suspended from above. As they reached the far end, the guard turned and pointed out his new accommodations: a cell bearing two steel-framed cots and one stainless steel toilet/sink combo for the two inmates to share. The pungent odor of bleach confirmed the cell was recently cleaned, probably in anticipation of his arrival. He chose the empty bunk on the right, flung the mat across the steel ribs and dropped the blanket across the bottom of the bed.

As he flopped down onto the bed, Jeremy interlaced his fingers behind his head as the guard slid the door shut and called out a command over the radio that locked the door from a secret location.

All was quiet. As he lay upon the bed and let his mind begin to wonder who might fill the empty rack next to him, Jeremy inspected his confined space. That's when a little black shadow under the other bunk caught his eye. Intrigued at his find, Jeremy sat straight up to try to identify the object from his seated position in bed. *The guards know better than to leave stuff in a cell.* He tilted his head with an inquisitive look. Unable to conclude what the item might be, he became curious. As he looked out the window of his cell door, Jeremy didn't notice any officials in the area and decided he could check out this item without any repercussions. Jeremy scooted to the edge of the bunk, squatted down on his hands and knees, and reached under the empty bed frame.

It's a book. I wonder how it got here?

The dark hardback cover was bare; the book had been discarded under the cot landing on its face. As Jeremy flipped it over, he saw the words, "HOLY BIBLE" faintly inscribed across the front in gold. He blew the dirt from the books' spine and swiped it with his sleeve, almost out of a sense of respect. As he sat on the edge of his bed, he thumbed through a great deal of pages until his eyes caught the heading of one of the books.

John.

###

Coming soon…

death comes uninvited
THE LAST PAGES OF A HOMICIDE DETECTIVE'S NOTEBOOK

CHAPTER ONE

Small waves lapped softly against the splintered bulkhead as the late evening's full moon glistened against the edges of each ripple as it worked its way towards the shore. A cool breeze stirred from the southern portion of the peninsula and wound its way up along the beach line and swirled into the night club's windows. The River Shack was the new party hot spot for those who had just acquired the required legal drinking age but had not yet found the maturity to handle the responsibility needed to keep them from plunging into utter stupidity. The dance floor and bar areas were filled beyond capacity, something the owner had not experienced in a good while. The owner surveyed the crowd as he finished wiping down a glass; he searched for the source of his sudden financial success. After all, it was the third Friday night in a row his taps were ran nearly dry and his young clientele begged for more.

The gray planked walls, adorned with aged life rings, rowing oars and other long forgotten maritime relics gave the ambience of an old classic fishing trawler just in from a wharf off of the coast of Maine. In the far corner just beneath a flickering iron gas lantern, a group of young men sat and glared at one another in disgust. They cupped their hands around their mugs and spoke to each other only with darting eyes. Raul lifted his mug and chugged the last of his lukewarm ale, slammed the glass back onto the rustic table while he gave a quick sideways nod with his head. It was time to make their move.

Each of the six Hispanic men tried to finish as much of his remaining beer in the few seconds allotted them as they slid out from the corner booth and squeezed in tightly together and worked their way across the crowded dance floor. Bodies pressed against them from every direction as the carefree partiers swiveled and swayed to the rhythmic beats that blared across the cramped room.

Raul glanced back to Julio. The countenance scribbled across his face told Julio precisely who had brought him to his agitation. Everyday respect was something to be commanded, not earned. With a second distinct jerk of his head, Raul motioned to Julio who turned back and gave a quick series of hand signals to his compadres. The associates quickly encircled the group of guys who stood near the wooden support post as they drank their replenished beer.

"Yo, bitch," Raul yelled.

James heard someone scream something just over the music and looked to his left, beer in hand, and saw the Hispanic subject who had been eyeballing him all night.

"What?" James yelled back and smirked at the scouring man.

"I got something for you bitch," Raul yelled as he raised the Glock 27 semi-auto handgun over his head and began pouring rounds down into the group of men. As he jerked the trigger in rapid succession, Raul counted his shots; he knew he needed to save one last round before he fled.

Panic and hysteria erupted in the River Shack and poured through the doors and windows into the parking lot. Intoxicated patrons fled for their lives as they scrambled for the safety of their cars.

"That's for disrespecting me," Raul said and walked towards his wounded prey as he raised the Glock one last time.

With careful aim, he aligned the sights straight at James' head and squeezed the trigger, "...and that's to make sure you don't pull that shit again!"

James' body fell limp as bright red blood poured from his wound and spilled onto the scuffed wooden flooring. Others, wounded by the stampede, had avoided being scathed by any of the stray rounds. As these terrified patrons crawled towards safety, Raul and his five amigos ran out the door, jumped into their decrepit Cadillac and sped away from the scene.

****

It was a skeleton crew tasked to carry out the responsibilities of the three-to-eleven shift that Friday night, With only thirty minutes left to finish their shift, three detectives sat patiently waiting for the minutes to tick off the clock. Lang thumbed through his attaché folder and ensured there were plenty of the proper forms that may be needed for this weekend's on-call duty. Jones and Stanton sat quietly at their desks and cleared up the last remnants of their most recent murderous escapade as they shuffled papers into the file and scooted it to the desks' edge. "Anyone up for a beer at the Green Turtle tonight?" Stanton asked.

"Sorry, but I start on-call in about twenty-eight minutes," Lang said as he checked his wristwatch.

"Wish I could," said Jones, "but I've got to get up early tomorrow for a 'family function,'" he said while using his fingers to make quote signs in midair.

"Oh yeah, and what kind of family adventure do you have tomorrow, Jonesy?" asked Lang.

"My wife's cousin is getting married. If I could miss it, I would," Jones said.

As the banter between the detectives continued, the phone rang. Jones saw his opportunity to escape the harassing friendly fire and snatched the receiver to evade the torment. Stanton swiveled around in his chair to assess the incoming phone call as Jones had said little past the initial greeting and was intently scribbling notes down into his reporter style notebook.

"This better not interfere with me purging the ol' tap," Stanton said.

Jones hung up the receiver, pulled his handheld radio out from his bag, flipped the switches and tuned in to the police broadcast from the Fourteenth District.

"No, no, no; this isn't happening!" Stanton snapped, seeing his as his hopes for some cold suds evaporated before his eyes.

"They had a shooting at the River Shack; some Hispanic guy lit up this black dude's ass. He's 10-7, pronounced at the scene. The district guys are holding some witnesses who know who the shooter is, so grab your shit and let's get moving!"

****

The 10:45 p.m. gridlock proved to be a sight never seen before by any member within the agency. Even the old timers stood with their hands on their hips in complete amazement. *I've never seen the likes of this before, not in all my years.* Yet, as the detectives squeezed their unmarked vehicles into a small and remote corner of the parking lot, they focused their attention on a small group of people huddled just outside the door of the establishment.

"Detective, over here," cried out one officer.

"This is Stacy; you might want to talk with her. Says she didn't actually see the shooting but knows what happened."

"I see," said Jones, "and you know what happened because you know the parties involved, I'm guessing?"

"Yeah, we all went to school together a few years ago," she said bleary-eyed from tears that still welled up. "James was a really nice guy; just a year older than me. He was here with a bunch of friends and started having some problems with two guys, Carlos and Julio, who also went to school with me. They were giving James a bunch of shit about something."

"Well, usually these things are over girls or drugs. Either of those in play tonight?" Jones asked.

"I'm not really sure. I don't know them like that. I just know there was some tension between James and the two guys. Then this other guy came over and just started shooting."

"I thought you didn't see the shooting?"

"I didn't, but I did see a third guy come over." Stacy paused, taking in the memories of those terrifying moments and finding it difficult to hold back her emotions. She could still hear the erratic popping sound that had sent everyone scurrying in all directions and seeking any inanimate object that would provide them some level of safety.

"All of a sudden everybody was running towards the doors, some were even jumping out of windows. I thought they were going to shoot us all," she said as she crinkled the tissue and dabbed her eyes.

"Do you know who the shooter was?" ask Jones.

"No, I had never seen him before; all I know is that he was a friend of Carlos and Julio," she explained.

"Okay, we'll need to make sure that we have your information and–" Jones went on to explain the detectives may need to get back in touch with her and perhaps have her look through some yearbooks they had access to through the Board of Education.

While Jones addressed the witnesses, Stanton and Lang entered the shadowy tavern and strained to peer into the far reaches of the darkness. Lang pulled the seven-inch metal shaft from his jacket pocket, clicked the button, and suddenly 11,000 candela of light streamed across the darkened plain. Though it was more compact than the longer and bulkier metallic flashlights Lang remembered using much like a nightstick while in patrol, the intensity of the newly advanced flashlights was almost overwhelming. Lang's light glided back and forth as the two detectives cautiously ambled across the room like a single spotlight that surveyed the black felt curtain draped over a stage in anticipation of the next performer.

The dark shadowy lump that lay on the floor just behind the wood encased pillar caught both detectives' eyes as they zeroed in on what would soon be determined to be the substance of the crime scene. The detectives hovered at a distance and scanned the floor with their flashlights as they searched for casings, bloodstains, and possible shoe prints left by the suspect on the dusty floor.

The department's newly acquired shoe and tire impression software had seen recent success in the crime lab as technicians were identifying the make of particular shoe impressions left at some recent robbery scenes. As these achievements were clearing a number of cases in other units in the Criminal Investigation Division, Stanton was chomping at the bit to see this advanced technology at work. But, with the hundreds of intoxicated young adults who went sprinting across the floor when the lead was flying, it would be an insurmountable task to lift each of the shoe impressions and determine which of the hundreds belonged to the actual shooter. Additionally, short of having the actual shoe to compare with an actual impression, crime lab technicians wouldn't be able to link the impression to any particular person. However, as the detectives continued to let their flashlights glide across the floor, the dull glint from the pile of casings lying some fifteen feet from the cooling cadaver left the detectives with an expectation the case would yield more tangible evidence through a regiment of ballistic analyses.

Stanton let out a deep sigh as he finished surveying the work that needed done. "Tell you what, because you've got the on-call this weekend, I'll take this one. I'll document the shooting scene; if you can get the rest of the bar that would be great!"

"Sure thing. Have you seen crime lab yet?" Lang asked.

"No, they were in the middle of shift change when the call came out and with all the bottlenecked cars out there I'm sure they'll be a while getting here." Stanton frowned, as he wished he was at his chosen establishment sucking down a cold one.

****

Police cruisers with their red and blue strobe lights streaming deep into the darkness of the night surrounded the River Shack and entrapped anyone who had not made it out of the parking lot. Uniformed officers were netting in witnesses and securing their handwritten statements at the makeshift roadblock every guest would have to funnel through in order to depart the nightmare. In turn, each car approached the officers who secured valid forms of identification and issued blank statement forms that were soon completed by the occupants and returned. As the officers waited for the witnesses to author their memoir of the murder, criminal records checks were quietly conducted in the background trying to ensure a probable suspect wasn't being overlooked. With the wanted checks coming back negative and the statements completed, the district officers soon found that the parking lot was nearly empty as the mountain of information piled high on the hood of the cruiser.

****

The yellow measuring tape stretched from the far corner of the room as Laura Pennington pulled it tight and looked down at the number falling exactly center over the victim's nose. "Twenty three feet, seven and a half inches," she said aloud while making the notation on her diagram. Again and again she repeated the process until she had measured each of the victim's extremities, head and torso. After she recorded the numbers that would permit her to recreate the scene to scale in a formal courtroom proceeding, Pennington carefully stepped around the puddle of dried blood and began the same process for each of the casings, duly noting the exact position where each fell and how it landed.

"With the casings lying right here, your boy had to be standing somewhere over here," Lang estimated after completing his notes from his earlier assignment of documenting the bar.

"Think we should look for shoe prints?" Stanton asked.

Lang shrugged his shoulders and thought, *Why not?* "Couldn't hurt."

The detectives retrieved their handy illumination tools and saturated the floor with the intense beams of light. Lang knelt down looking hard at the floor at an angle that prevented the glare from overwhelming textures left behind on the floor.

"Looks like a lot of shoe prints. Some are smudged, others aren't. Do you want Laura to try and lift the ones that only reflect extreme details?" Lang asked Stanton.

Pennington busily continued working on her crime scene diagram in spite of overhearing the two detectives who were conjuring up more work she felt would most likely prove to be fruitless. She began to think about what she could say that would dissuade the investigators from insisting on the shoe print lifts. Pennington mulled over her words. As she began to formulate her argument she overheard the chatter on her radio that quickly reminded her how busy the remaining forensic technicians who were handling all of the other calls for service while she was tied up on the murder. She thought carefully how she could be inundated with processing calls and soon realized taking the extra time to lift the shoe prints might not be a bad idea after all. *Think I'll stay right here*, she thought as she finished her last few measurements and prepared to lift half a dozen shoe prints.

****

The investigators had pressed on well into the early morning hours before the transport service arrived to bag James' remains and transport him downtown to the medical examiners office in preparation for the autopsy in just a few short hours. Saturday mornings always proved to be a more convenient day for a visit to the morgue because the downtown clamor of traffic was usually nonexistent. A quick ride and readily available parking out front made the day a little more pleasurable considering the task which brought the investigators to the morgue in the first place.

Dr. Sorina Pavel walked into the mortared examination room and grabbed the roll call sheet from the corner of the countertop mounted immediately next to the doorway. Dr. Pavel perused the list of those who had recently departed this earth and how they met their demise before she glanced at the motor vehicle accidents, suicides, and suspicious deaths. She identified those who were murdered and needed a doctor specifically assigned to conduct the examination.

"Detective Stanton, how are you on this beautiful Saturday

morning?" she asked.

Stanton, who was half slumped over on the stool while the doctors were conducting their morning roll call ritual, sat up, rubbed his bleary eyes, and gave an innocent shrug of the shoulders to suggest he was here and wasn't real happy about it.

"Ah, I see, someone's been up all night," Pavel said with a smirk. "Let me see what I can do about getting your guy started and done so you can go home and get some rest."

"Go home? Not on this one, Doc. We've got some leads on a suspect I've got to start tracking down after I'm done here."

"Tell you what, I'll personally handle your case and see to it that you're back at your office in the next few hours. How does that sound?"

"Great, but that still doesn't get me home," Stanton jested, able to form a slight grin.

****

Lang and Jones poured through the cellphone records that were spitting off of the fax machine in record time. The fifty-seven page report along with the 282-page supplemental report and tower information were eating up a lot of paper and time. With the reports strewn across the conference table strategically positioned in the center of the office, Lang and Jones organized the information and deducted which of the phone numbers may have belonged to the killer's associates.

"It looks like the victim was getting some harassing calls long before getting to the River Shack. According to one witness, he was getting some annoying calls around 7:00 last night but didn't end up at the bar until sometime after 9:00," Jones said.

Lang raised his eyes from the exorbitant amount of reports. "Well, what about earlier in the day? His calling pattern should show when his phone went active, usually starting with reaching out to people he knows."

"Yeah, but this guy lives on his phone, look at all these

calls. I don't think I use my phone this much in a week, let alone a day!" Jones reached up and undid his tie and top shirt button, frustrated and exhausted.

"Let's do this: lets sort out the phone numbers and see which ones call the least amount of times. After that we'll look to see if any of them fall around 7:00. That should tell us how many times these knuckleheads called the victim and give us some indication how well the victim may have known the killer," Lang suggested.

The detectives returned their attention to the record details and plotted each of the phone numbers on a yellow legal pad as they sorted through the information.

"It's really hard to say which of these numbers could be the harassing numbers--short of calling them, it's hard to eliminate them," said Jones.

Lang pushed back from the table and lumbered over to his desk where the stack of written statements was sprawled out. After he gathered them into a pile, Lang returned to the conference table; one by one he correlated the cell phone numbers provided by those who had completed the statements to the unknown numbers listed on the call details. Having identified nearly all of the unknown numbers, Lang took the remaining ones, researched their carriers and typed out the court order request for their subscriber information. Able to articulate an exigency request, Lang finished the required paperwork and shot off the requests to the individual carriers through the fax machine.

Since the flurry of investigative activity surrounding James' cellphone activity had begun before the crack of dawn, Lang and Jones decided to take a break and head out to grab something that would help alleviate the hunger pangs now bearing on them.

"You up for the diner?" asked Jones.

"Do you mean am I up for a stack of blueberry pancakes, bacon, scrambled eggs and some fresh coffee—you bet," Lang said with the mere thought of food rejuvenating his energy.

The diner was just minutes away from the office, so Lang and Jones quickly jumped into the car and secured a front row parking spot in the diner's lot. They nearly sprinted in through the glass doors and took up residency in a far corner booth away from any prying ears.

"You might want to keep your ears open around the office and be careful with what you say," warned Jones.

"What do you mean, Jonesy? What's going on?"

"Well, let's just say I heard from a little birdie that Metzger is in deep shit. I'm not sure exactly what's going on, but I've been hearing some murmurings about some, shall we say— entanglements."

"Big deal, that isn't anything new with him. He's always into something."

"Evidently this one is pretty serious. The sergeant has been conversing with some internal affairs people as well as commanders. I'm not sure this is going to shake out too well for Metzger, but it might work out really well for the squad if we can get a replacement worth his weight in gold," Jones said.

Lang weighed the information as the waitress placed the steaming hot mugs of coffee in front of the two detectives who politely waited for their privacy to be restored before resuming their conversation.

"Yeah, but we all know that Metzger is the golden child, the favorite one. He's like Teflon, nothing ever sticks," Lang explained.

"I don't know; I think this one does," Jones said, raising his eyebrow with emphasis.

"Then you know more than you're willing to tell," countered Lang with a wry grin.

The expression on Jones' face confirmed Lang's accusation, though Jones continued to hesitate about revealing the information he had acquired. He drew his fingers around his chin in deep contemplation and carefully considered his next words.

"I'll say this—I think that there is a good possibility that Metzger is ousted from the unit despite what everyone thinks about him being like Teflon."

"But it doesn't make sense. He's always having problems with side-stepping the rules and regulations and is never charged or held accountable for his actions. He's one of these guys who got into the unit, not because of his investigative skills—we know he doesn't have any—but because he was friends with homicide detectives back in the day. Now that they are all gone, he's still here and floundering. When he gets an investigation, he does little if anything to chase down his leads, and then throws it on the shelf waiting for some miracle to happen. Then as fate would have it, he gets some dumb lucky break. And it's not from anything he's done; he's just got a horseshoe stuck up his ass. One minute he's got a cold case sitting on the shelf, and the next, he's got some anonymous caller on the phone saying 'Oh, by the way, so and so killed such and such!' In all my career I've never seen any detective in any unit clear so many cases with such dumb luck," Lang said.

Jones sat quietly, shaking his head in agreement, sharing Lang's frustrations.

"You know exactly what I'm talking about. I've never seen anything like it. This guy is the commander's favorite. If a team gets a murder and a new team needs to be put on call, Petrelli always orders me to go on call and says that 'Metzger has something to do this weekend.' Like *I* don't? I'm always having to pick up the on-call and cover for people while Metzger gets to sit around home, watch the Ravens and eat bonbons or whatever it is he does," Lang said.

"I understand what you're saying, Ken, but I'm telling you, I don't think Metzger will survive this one. There's a good chance his recent actions just very well may have him criminally charged, if not charged with malfeasance of office."

Silence fell over the detectives just as the waitress stepped up to the table's edge, plates in hand. "Which one of you guys ordered the blueberry pancakes?"

###

CPSIA information can be obtained at www.ICGtesting.com
Printed in the USA
LVOW11s1318141214

418773LV00002B/281/P

KEN LANG STUDIOS

Find more great books like this at www.KenLangStudios.c

Connect with Ken
Email: kenlangstudios@gmail.com
Twitter: @DetKenLang
Facebook: www.facebook.com/detkenlang